Cambridge Elements ≡

Elements in Perception
edited by
James T. Enns
The University of British Columbia

ECOLOGICAL PSYCHOLOGY

Miguel Segundo-Ortin
University of Murcia

Vicente Raja
University of Murcia

CAMBRIDGE
UNIVERSITY PRESS

Shaftesbury Road, Cambridge CB2 8EA, United Kingdom

One Liberty Plaza, 20th Floor, New York, NY 10006, USA

477 Williamstown Road, Port Melbourne, VIC 3207, Australia

314–321, 3rd Floor, Plot 3, Splendor Forum, Jasola District Centre,
New Delhi – 110025, India

103 Penang Road, #05–06/07, Visioncrest Commercial, Singapore 238467

Cambridge University Press is part of Cambridge University Press & Assessment,
a department of the University of Cambridge.

We share the University's mission to contribute to society through the pursuit of
education, learning and research at the highest international levels of excellence.

www.cambridge.org
Information on this title: www.cambridge.org/9781009451406

DOI: 10.1017/9781009451413

© Miguel Segundo-Ortin and Vicente Raja 2024

This publication is in copyright. Subject to statutory exception and to the provisions
of relevant collective licensing agreements, no reproduction of any part may take
place without the written permission of Cambridge University Press & Assessment.

When citing this work, please include a reference to the DOI 10.1017/9781009451413

First published 2024

A catalogue record for this publication is available from the British Library.

ISBN 978-1-009-45140-6 Hardback
ISBN 978-1-009-45136-9 Paperback
ISSN 2515-0502 (online)
ISSN 2515-0499 (print)

Additional resources for this publication at www.cambridge.org/Miguel_Vicente

Cambridge University Press & Assessment has no responsibility for the persistence
or accuracy of URLs for external or third-party internet websites referred to in this
publication and does not guarantee that any content on such websites is, or will
remain, accurate or appropriate.

Ecological Psychology

Elements in Perception

DOI: 10.1017/9781009451413
First published online: March 2024

Miguel Segundo-Ortin
University of Murcia

Vicente Raja
University of Murcia

Author for correspondence: Miguel Segundo-Ortin, miguel.segundo@um.es

Abstract: Ecological psychology is one of the main alternative theories of perception and action available in the contemporary literature. This Element explores and analyzes its most relevant ideas, concepts, methods, and experimental results. It first discusses the historical roots of the ecological approach. The Element then analyzes the works of the two main founders of ecological psychology: James and Eleanor Gibson. It also explores the development of ecological psychology since the 1980s until nowadays. Finally, the Element identifies and evaluates the future of the ecological approach to perception and action.

Keywords: affordances, direct perception, embodied cognition, J. J. Gibson, E. J. Gibson

© Miguel Segundo-Ortin and Vicente Raja 2024

ISBNs: 9781009451406 (HB), 9781009451369 (PB), 9781009451413 (OC)
ISSNs: 2515-0502 (online), 2515-0499 (print)

Contents

Introduction

Ecological psychology was originally formulated in the works of James and Eleanor Gibson. Since then, the ecological approach has become a scientific framework that provides an alternative to mainstream theories of perception and **perceptual learning** within experimental psychology and cognitive science. In this Element we will explore and analyze the most relevant conceptual and methodological moves that led toward ecological psychology as well as the subsequent developments in the field up to the present.

For now though, it is worth noting that James and Eleanor Gibson's overall aim was to explain all aspects of perception and perceptual learning without invoking nonperceptual, cognitive resources of any kind. In a world still dominated by the behaviorist stimulus–response arc but already witnessing a change toward the notions of computation and representation typical of cognitive psychology, they offered a third path. As James Gibson (1967[1982]) put it:

> We [James and Eleanor Gibson] have no patience with the attempt to patch up the S–R [stimulus–response] formula with hypotheses of mediation [e.g., mental representations]. In behavior theory as well as in psychophysics you either find causal relations or you do not. (p. 12)

Most mainstream theories of perception and perceptual learning since at least the time of Helmholtz have relied on different forms of psychological mediators. Unconscious inferences, homunculi, brain regions with psychological powers or computational capacities; all these have been postulated to mediate between stimuli and responses in order to explain perceptual experience and behavior. James and Eleanor Gibson tried to avoid this explanatory strategy and, to do so, embraced a simple but powerful hypothesis: there are aspects of stimulation, however complex, that enable perceptual experience, the perceptual control of action, and perceptual learning without the need for mediatory processes. This hypothesis is at the core of ecological psychology, and it is also the seed of notions like **direct perception**, **ecological information**, and **affordance**.

After exploring the historical roots of the ecological approach to perception and action in Section 1, in Section 2 we will dive deeper into the ways James and Eleanor Gibson developed its core hypotheses and concepts. In Section 3, we will explore how ecological psychology has evolved over the last few decades, giving rise to a series of solid research programs. Finally, in Section 4 we will review the current state of the ecological approach to perception and action and its future directions. After the four sections, we offer a succinct Glossary with the most important concepts used throughout the Element.

Before starting, however, we must warn the reader that purely philosophical discussions, like the ontological nature of affordances and the ecologically inspired arguments against mental representations are kept to a bare minimum, although we do not deny their importance. Indeed, a proof of their relevance is the extensive attention they have received in the literature (e.g., Chemero, 2009; Heras-Escribano, 2019). However, had we included them, they would have been a distraction from the main aim of this Element: to provide a systematic account of ecological psychology as a scientific framework full of lively research programs.

1 The Historical Roots of Ecological Psychology

The first step in order to get a full picture of ecological psychology is to acknowledge its historical roots. To do so, we will review the core ideas of American functionalism, radical empiricism, **Gestalt** psychology, and some forms of behaviorism. All these ideas played a crucial role in the education of James and Eleanor Gibson, and many of their core tenets were at the basis of the ecological approach to perception and action. Some of these tenets include that certain aspects of stimulation can lead to perception without mediatory processes, that perception–action loops must be treated as indivisible units, and the focus on the active character of perception and experience.

1.1 American Functionalism and Radical Empiricism

The path toward ecological psychology began with the academic career of James Gibson. He obtained his PhD at Princeton University under the supervision of psychologist H. S. Langfeld and the mentorship of psychologist E. B. Holt. Holt's influence was crucial to him during his formative years to the extent that he described himself as a "radical empiricist, like Holt" in his autobiography (J. J. Gibson, 1967[1982], p. 12). It was during these years that James Gibson got exposed to American functionalism and, evidently, radical empiricism. And it was during this time that some ideas from these two frameworks got into his own thinking.

Before behaviorism took over the psychological sciences in around the 1920s, American functionalism – or just functionalism – was one of the main frameworks within experimental psychology. Notably related to the ideas of William James and John Dewey, it was named 'functionalism' as opposed to 'structuralism,' defended by the prominent psychologist Edward Titchener (1898). Structuralism was concerned with the identification and analysis of the building blocks of experience; for instance, the identification and study of simple sensations as the elementary components of perceptual processes. Once these building blocks are known, so the story goes, we will be able to find the processes and rules that merge them into different psychological structures. Against this approach, functionalism characterized the task of psychology as the identification and study of psychological functions and took the building blocks of experience described by structuralists to be artifacts of their research logic and methods. In fact, functionalists claimed that the focus on such building blocks was an obstacle for the study of psychological functions and events as unified wholes. William James' critique of simple sensations is a perfect illustration of this view:

> Most books start with sensations, as the simplest mental facts, and proceed synthetically, constructing each higher stage from those below it. But this is abandoning the empirical method of investigation. *No one ever had a simple sensation by itself.* Consciousness, from our natal day, is of a teeming multiplicity of objects and relations, and what we call simple sensations are results of discriminative attention, pushed often to a very high degree. (James, 1890, Vol. 1, p. 224; emphasis added)

In their critique of structuralism, functionalists do not only regard simple sensations as theoretical artifacts but also call into question the whole stimulus–response structure – aka *reflex arc*. Dewey (1896) thought that the characterization of psychological events as chains of atomic stimuli that trigger atomic responses was a misguided attempt to capture those events. Only after a response is triggered, Dewey argues, can an environmental feature be meaningfully described as a stimulus. Even more, the very notion of a triggered response is inadequate, for only already-active organisms are in the position of registering, identifying, and coordinating with those environmental events called 'stimuli.' Dewey famously appealed to James' example of a child and a candle to exemplify this point:

> The ordinary interpretation [of a child-candle grasping situation] would say the sensation of light is a stimulus to the grasping as a response, the burn resulting is a stimulus to withdrawing the hand as response and so on . . . Upon analysis, we find that we begin not with a sensory stimulus, but with a sensorimotor coordination, the optical-ocular, and that in a certain sense *it is the movement which is primary, and the sensation which is secondary*, the movement of body, head and eye muscles determining the quality of what is experienced. In other words, *the real beginning is with the act of seeing; it is looking, and not a sensation of light.* (Dewey, 1896, p. 358–359; emphasis added)

Psychological events are thus described in terms of coordinated, organic circuits in which elementary components only make sense within the particular context of the whole system. Regarding one or another part of the circuit as primary or secondary – or as stimulus or response – is just a way to arbitrarily break the whole event for some explanatory purpose. Dewey's point is that, while the ordinary interpretation of the child-candle situation is that it starts with the sensation of light, it is perfectly possible to set its beginning in the optical-ocular sensorimotor coordination. There is no principled way to set the beginning or the end of a psychological event when it is taken to be an organic circuit. The whole is ontologically and epistemologically primary.

In this context, if the organic circuit is the starting point of any psychological explanation, a structuralist research logic based on the primacy of component identification seems deeply misguided. This radical idea stayed within the repertoire of James and Eleanor Gibson for the rest of their careers and was central for the development of ecological psychology. Both their criticism of the notion of stimulus in psychology and their defense of perception–action loops as indivisible units reflect the functionalist inheritance of the ecological approach.

But this is not the only aspect in which American functionalism influenced James and Eleanor Gibson. William James proposed the hypothesis that whatever is given in sensation is more complex than what was acknowledged by the psychophysicists and physiologists of his time. In an argument often repeated in *The principles of psychology* (1890) that afterwards became the keystone of radical empiricism, James claims that sensations are not just atomic events but that there are sensations of *relations* between different aspects of the world. In the *Principles*, James (1890) says:

> If there be such things as feelings [i.e., sensations] at all, then so surely as relations between objects exist in *rerum naturâ*, so surely, and more surely, do feelings exist to which these relations are known . . . We ought to say a feeling of and, a feeling of if, a feeling of but, and a feeling of by, quite as readily as we say a feeling of blue or a feeling of cold. (Vol. 1, pp. 245–246; emphasis in the original)

Similarly, when he writes on radical empiricism, he says that "*the relations that connect experiences must themselves be experienced relations, and any kind of relation experienced must be accounted as 'real' as anything else in the system*" (James, 1904[1987], p. 1160; emphasis in the original).

The view that relations are directly experienced entailed the rejection of some of the principles of psychophysics and physiology and required a completely new understanding of experience. A good illustration of these consequences is James' critique of Helmholtz's theory of spatial perception. In general, James thought that any process of inference that went from simple sensations to complex experiences was untenable or just "pure mythology" (James, 1890, Vol. 1, p. 170), but he was especially blunt in the context of spatial perception. Helmholtz's theory began with simple sensations without spatial properties; namely, simple sensations that tell us nothing about location, direction, and so on. These simple sensations were then associated to construct the perceived spatial properties by a process of *unconscious inference*. In this context, James (1890) asks:

> But how, it may be asked, can association produce a space-quality not in the things associated? How can we by induction or analogy infer what we do not already generically know? Can 'suggestions of experience' reproduce elements which no particular experience originally contained? This is the point by which Helmholtz's 'empiristic' theory, as a theory, must be judged. No theory is worthy of the name which leaves such a point obscure. Well, Helmholtz does so leave it. At one time he seems to fall back on inscrutable powers of the soul, and to range himself with the 'psychical stimulists'. He speaks of Kant as having made the essential step in the matter in distinguishing the content of experience from that form – space, course – which is given it by the peculiar faculties of the mind. (Vol. 1, p. 279)

According to James, Helmholtz's explanatory strategy ultimately relied on some form of obscure a priori knowledge – the "inscrutable powers of the soul" – the origins and structure of which remained unjustified and mysterious. To use James Gibson's words, such a priori knowledge serves to patch up the stimulus–response formula with some mediatory, inferential steps that help transforming simple sensations with no spatial properties whatsoever into full-fledged perceptual experiences of space. William James never wanted to appeal to such inferences for, as we have seen, he regarded them as mostly mythological. James and Eleanor Gibson shared this feeling, and both pursued a Jamesian solution to avoid mediatory inferences, accepting the complexity of experience and the richness of stimuli to support it. As an American functionalist and a radical empiricist, William James' fundamental commitment was that sensations are rich enough to provide us not just with the experience of simple events but also of their relations.[1] James and Eleanor Gibson inherited this radical hypothesis and developed it into a scientific theory: the ecological approach to perception and action.

1.2 Gestalt Psychology (and Phenomenology)

Although the Jamesian influence was there from the very beginning through the mentorship of Holt (a student of William James himself; see Heft, 2001), James and Eleanor Gibson took some time to fully develop a scientific theory compatible with the core hypotheses of American functionalism and radical empiricism. Indeed, a little detour was needed.

---

[1] The relationship between stimulation and sensation can be problematized. However, James' use of "sensation", and sometimes "feeling," is mostly a matter of preference. The differences with James and Eleanor Gibson's use of "stimulation" are not relevant for the compatibility of their positions.

In 1928, James Gibson was hired to teach experimental psychology at Smith College (Northampton, MA, USA). Moving to Smith College was crucial for him, first of all, because there he met Eleanor (who was his student), eventually married her, and began a lifelong, shared intellectual quest within experimental psychology (E. J. Gibson, 2001). And second, because he became an academic fellow of Kurt Koffka, the prominent gestalt psychologist. Although he wrote his dissertation against Gestalt psychology, the exposure to Koffka's thinking and, later, to gestalt theory and philosophical phenomenology more generally made an important mark on James Gibson. By the end of his life, he even claimed the ecological approach was "a sort of *ecological* Gestalt theory" (J. J. Gibson, 1979[1982], p. 112).

Gestalt psychology is a theoretical framework developed by psychologists Max Wertheimer, Kurt Koffka, and Wolfgang Köhler in Germany and Austria in the early twentieth century (see Ash, 1995; Koffka, 1935; Wagemans et al., 2012). Like American functionalists and radical empiricists, gestalt psychologists rejected the structuralist explanatory strategy based on the identification of simple sensations. According to them, perceptual experience has formal features (or gestalts) that go beyond the addition or association of elementary components. For instance, we see groups, series, or some figures for which we do not have any sensation (Figure 1). Thus, gestalts cannot be reduced to the association or combination of simple sensations: there is no way to find simple sensations for groups, series, or some figures along with typical simple sensations like "dot", "hard", or "blue." Gestalt psychologists then faced the same dichotomy William James identified in Helmholtz's theory of spatial perception: if our perceptual experience includes elements that are not given in the form of simple sensations, we are forced to either postulate some obscure a priori knowledge or to find a different solution to explain such experience.

Gestalt psychologists found a physiological solution for this issue. Instead of proposing a mediatory, psychological process such as an unconscious inference, they gestured toward laws of self-organization of brain activity. In this context, "self-organization" has to do with the spontaneous activity of the brain that reaches some ordered state (a gestalt) given some stimulation. As cited by Stadler and Kruse (1990), Wolfgang Köhler describes this process in terms of the achievement of "stationary equilibrium distributions developed from the inner dynamics of the optical system itself" (p. 34). In other words, we perceive gestalts because our brain is the way it is, and its dynamics self-organize the way they do. Thus, gestalt psychologists rehearse a solution different from the structuralist one but also different from the one proposed by American functionalists; whereas American functionalists endorsed the hypothesis that the

Figure 1 Examples of gestalts in visual perception. For instance,
an all-white triangle for which no simple sensation is available (1st row, 3rd
figure left to right), an all-white sphere in the origin of the thorns for which no
simple sensation is available (2nd row, 2nd figure left to right),
or a grouping by similarity for which no simple sensation is available (3rd row,
3rd figure left to right). (Copyright holder: Impronta, CC BY-SA 3.0 – Source.
www.interaction-design.org/literature/topics/gestalt-principles; accessed
March 31, 2022.)

richness of sensations is enough to support perceptual experience, gestalt
psychologists opted for a solution based on intrinsic brain dynamics.

From this point of view, it is not surprising that James Gibson attached the
adjective "ecological" when he claimed his own theory was a sort of gestalt
theory. He generally agreed with the critique of simple sensations and mediatory
processes. Also, he valued the general move toward understanding perceptual
experience in terms of complex holistic structures (gestalts) and self-
organization. However, he thought such self-organization should not be found
just in the brain alone but, as we will see, in the whole ecological, organism–
environment system. The influence of Gestalt psychology in the ecological
approach to perception and action was therefore not a matter of James and
Eleanor Gibson embracing gestalt theory as such, but worked more as a ladder

to streamline and complement their functionalist tendencies. Gestalt psychology provided them with further arguments against the understanding of experience as the product of adding simple sensations together.

The general influence of gestalt theory in ecological psychology lasted all the way up to the final works of James Gibson and beyond. Indeed, James Gibson was explicit about this influence many times. In addition to considering the ecological approach as a sort of ecological gestalt theory, he also claimed, in a letter to his lifelong friend Gunnar Johansson, that what he was defending was that in a sense "there are Gestalt laws and not only for the brain, but also for light" (Gibson, 1970a/1982, p. 85). In a way, he was a realist about gestalts.

James Gibson also acknowledged the phenomenological psychologist Albert Michotte as a researcher who was generally pursuing a project similar to the ecological one (Gibson, 1967[1982]). Michotte was himself influenced by Gestalt psychology and phenomenology, and he was convinced that perceptual experience was richer than acknowledged by mainstream behaviorism. In his work, Michotte (1946) was primarily concerned with the perception of causality and defended that we perceive causes without the need for any kind of mediatory, cognitive inference. Such directness made causation a kind of gestalt and highlighted the reason why James Gibson thought of Michotte as an ally within experimental psychology. Finally, it is well known that James and Eleanor Gibson were influenced by the works of Maurice Merleau-Ponty, the French phenomenologist who was in turn greatly influenced by gestalt theory (Käufer & Chemero, 2015). The influence of Merleau-Ponty's phenomenology is most visible in the ecological characterization of perception as an embodied process (see Section 2.3).

1.3 The Other Behaviorism

We should not forget, however, that for most of their careers James and Eleanor Gibson identified themselves with some form of behaviorism. James Gibson was influenced by the works of E. B. Holt, and for Eleanor Gibson, Clark L. Hull was the most influential figure. Both Holt and Hull represented different forms of behaviorism that were nevertheless equally far from the somewhat cartoonish received view of the framework.

As history is usually written by the victors, in this case cognitive psychologists, behaviorism is often described as concerned with just simple stimulus–response loops, as neglecting any form of physiology or physiological work, as turning a blind eye to the active and spontaneous character of behavior, and so on. This description of most behaviorists is of course mostly inaccurate, and even mainstream ones like Edward Tolman or B. F. Skinner, would reject all these accusations.

This received view of behaviorism is even more misleading in the case of Holt and Hull. Holt was a radical empiricist in the theory and a behaviorist in the methods. He developed *molar behaviorism*: a lawful approach to behavior in which the mainstage is not for stimulus–response circuits, but for objects of the world and organized behavior considered as a coordinated totality: "[T]he fairly accurate description of [psychological] activity will invariably reveal a law (or laws) whereby this activity is shown to be a constant function of some aspect of the objective world" (Holt, 1915a, p. 370).

Moving away from the stimulus–response framework toward a more complex organism–environment relationship is a key property of the ecological approach to perception and action. But that's not all. Another important aspect of molar behaviorism is its focus on the intrinsically active character of behavior and experience. Instead of picturing cognitive systems as purely reactive machines, Holt leveraged a very peculiar interpretation of the Freudian notion of *wish* to account for their active character: "The *wish* is purpose embodied in the mechanism of all living organisms, that it is necessarily a wish about . . . some feature of the environment; so that a total situation comprising both *organism and environment* is always involved . . . Mind is a relation and not a substance" (Holt, 1915b, p. 99; emphasis in the original).

According to Holt, cognitive systems exhibit a form of intrinsic, endogenous organized activity that encompasses themselves and their environments. Crucially, both perceptual experience and behavior depend on this active nature. Similarly, in ecological psychology, the perception–action loop is unbreakable: action is as needed for perception as perception is needed for action. Even more, perception is regarded as an activity in itself and is taken to be always occurring in the context of the organism–environment system. Again, the Holtian influence is prominent in the ecological approach.

The works of Clark L. Hull do not feature within the mainstream of behavioristic psychology either. Hull proposed a nonstandard view of behavior within the behaviorist coordinates: a (self-proclaimed) *neo*behaviorist theory that aimed to explain learning and motivation from the laws of behavior. First and foremost, he viewed behavior as goal-directed. Namely, he viewed behavior not in terms of responses triggered by stimuli but in terms of purposeful actions driven by some need – aka Hull's *drive theory*. For him, behavior is spontaneous and intrinsically motivated by the needs of the organism. In this context, Hull takes learning to be based on the emergence and reinforcement of habits that respond to those needs.

Eleanor Gibson arrived at Hull's lab in 1934, after she was accepted as a PhD student at Yale University but was refused by Robert L. Yerkes because he did not allow women in his lab. During her PhD, she studied verbal learning by applying two of the classical principles of conditioning: generalization and differentiation. Indeed, she thought she had changed the scope of the two principles for good: "I felt that I had humanized the concepts of generalization and differentiation, taking them out of their original context of the conditioned reflex and using them as functional concepts for understanding problems of human learning. I must give Hull credit here (which he is seldom given) for wanting to do this very thing" (E. J. Gibson, 2001, p. 26).

The fact that she credits Hull for the humanization of generalization and differentiation is telling. Working with Hull allowed her to take well-established principles of conditioning and to change them into notions that do not need to be reduced to the discrimination or association of simple stimuli and simple responses. She was able to apply these principles to more general cognitive functions, like her general theory of perceptual learning, for instance – more on this in Section 2.5. From this point of view, the influence of Hull in the ecological approach is quite direct, at least as a mentor and catalyzer of Eleanor Gibson's ideas.

1.4 Dissident Psychophysics

The influences of American functionalism, radical empiricism, Gestalt psychology, phenomenology, and nonstandard forms of behaviorism leave us with James and Eleanor Gibson approaching the 1940s but not yet having ecological psychology in mind. So, what happened during the following years for the ecological approach to emerge? What triggered its development? Believe us or not, it was World War II.

During the decade before World War II, James Gibson started gaining relevance as a perceptual psychologist. He carried out several studies on topics like what became called "the Gibson effect" (J. J. Gibson, 1933) and the relationship between perception and driving (J. J. Gibson & Crooks, 1938). His academic status led to him being recruited by the US Army Air Force to develop a training program for prospective aviation pilots. He oversaw the creation of resources to teach pilots to take off, land, and so on, before they got to be in a real plane. To do so, he studied the nature of spatial perception in the context of aviation with the methods of classic psychophysics. Soon enough, James Gibson discovered that these methods were not adequate for the task he was recruited for, and that classic psychophysics was unhelpful to understand the relevant aspects of spatial perception for aviation. Shortly the realization became obvious: "I learned that when a science does not usefully apply to practical problems there is something wrong with the theory of the science" (J. J. Gibson, 1967[1982], p. 18). In the end, he crafted a series of videos, among other resources, to train aviation pilots. But these videos were not based on classic psychophysics anymore. The quest for practical knowledge to develop a training system for pilots ended up leading James Gibson to the construction of his own new perceptual theory.

The first steps of Gibson's new theory of perception were proposed in his book *The perception of the visual world* (J. J. Gibson, 1950a). The main idea of the book was what he named "perceptual psychophysics": a way to do psychophysics that, instead of looking for systematic relationships between simple stimuli and simple sensations, looks for systematic relationships between complex patterns of stimulation and perceptual experience. With perceptual psychophysics, James Gibson embraced the general psychophysical strategy of searching for a stimulus variable that relates to some property or quality of experience. However, instead of reducing that relationship to simple instances of the stimulus–response formula, he expanded the strategy to richer aspects of stimulation and perception as he was convinced that "there are laws relating perception to physical stimulation as well as laws relating it to physiological processes" (J. J. Gibson, 1950a, p. 8; see also Raja, 2019a).

Perceptual psychophysics already reflected the influence of American functionalism, radical empiricism, and Gestalt psychology. While classic psychophysics searched for stimulus–response relationships in the atomistic sense, perceptual psychophysics sought functional relationships between complex spatial and temporal aspects of stimulation (e.g., texture gradients, ordinal stimulation) and richer perceptual experiences (e.g., distance to an object, shapes of objects). As we will see, this insight will remain fundamental for the ecological approach to perception and action in terms of the *specification* relation between environmental properties and stimulus information.

Finding relationships between some higher-order properties of stimulation and perceptual experience allowed James Gibson to avoid mediatory processes of inference or enrichment to account for perception. The description of a direct relationship between stimulation and perception meant, at least according to him, that there is no need for a mental mechanism to connect them. Therefore, during the 1950s, he was closer to American functionalism and radical empiricism than to anything else (see Heft, 2001). He accepted the core idea of the richness of stimulation and began the pursual of a scientific theory of perception compatible with it. This pursual would eventually lead to the ecological approach, but one more step was needed. In *The perception of the visual world*, James Gibson still retained a classic assumption of perceptual theory: that the retinal image is the starting point of perception. However, both James and Eleanor Gibson soon realized that relying on retinal images produced unsolvable theoretical and experimental issues. Thus, the retinal image should be abandoned if they wanted to have a coherent theory of perception. That was the last move toward ecological psychology.

2 The Ecological Approach to Perception and Action: Theses, Concepts, and Methods

Their misgivings regarding the theoretical and empirical accuracy of the notion of the retinal image led James and Eleanor Gibson to develop an alternative approach to perception.[2] Their work culminated in the publication of dozens of papers and four major books: *The senses considered as perceptual systems* (J. J. Gibson, 1966), *Principles of perceptual learning and development* (E. J. Gibson, 1969), *The ecological approach to visual perception* (J. J. Gibson, 1979[2015]), and *An ecological approach to perceptual learning and development* (E. J. Gibson & Pick, 2000). The goal of this section is to present the key ideas of the ecological approach to perception and action as originally described by them. Before we proceed, however, we think it is important to give the reader a sense of what "ecological" means in this context.

Ecology studies the relationship between species and their environment. To do this, ecologists pay special attention to the way environmental changes affect living organisms and how living organisms interact with the aspects of their habitats that are meaningful for their survival and life goals. This strategy is reflected in two core ideas of ecological psychology. One is that perception evolved to allow organisms to act adaptively in their natural environments. The other core idea is that perceptual processes (as well as other psychological processes) occur along temporally extended periods of time in which organism and environment interact, reciprocally affecting each other. It follows from this second assumption that perception and other cognitive abilities cannot be explained by focusing on the organism alone. Instead, organism and environment constitute "an inseparable pair" (J. J. Gibson, 1979[2015], p. 4), a single unit often referred to as the "Organism–Environment [O-E] system" (Michaels & Carello, 1981; Turvey, 2019).

This ecological perspective is made clear in the first chapters of *The ecological approach to visual perception* (J. J. Gibson, 1979[2015]). There, James Gibson argues that any explanation of perception must begin with a description of the world scaled to the perceptual capabilities of the different organisms. He called this perceptual world "environment," in opposition to the "physical world," which encompasses everything .that exists, from atoms to galaxies: "We are concerned here with things at the ecological level, with the habitats

---

[2] See J. J. Gibson (1970b[1982]) for a detailed list of the anomalies he found regarding the notion of retinal image. For recent work on the problems of the retinal image, see Swanson (2015).

of animals and men, because we all behave with respect to things that we can look at and feel, or smell and taste, and events we can listen to" (p. 5).

The environment thus refers to the part of the physical world that organisms can be aware of and interact with, and it is properly described in ecological rather than physical terms. As we will show in this section, several key concepts in psychology (e.g., "information," "meaning," "development," and so on) are redefined once we adopt this ecological stance. Even the classical distinction between the mental (subjective) and the physical (objective) is rejected in favor of an ecological level of reality in which experience takes place.

2.1 Not Stimuli, but Information

Ecological psychology started with a criticism of the role attributed to stimuli in scientific explanations of perception. This criticism has two faces, one methodological and one theoretical. The methodological critique appears most clearly in a paper published by James Gibson (1960) entitled "The concept of the stimulus in psychology." In this paper, he conducted a systematic survey of how his peers used the notion of "stimulus." His conclusion was that the notion is inadequate for a scientific explanation of perception and behavior due to its many inconsistencies.

To begin with, whereas some researchers define a stimulus as whatever physical force that excites a receptor and initiates afferent neural impulses, others deny that stimuli alone suffice to cause such effects. Likewise, while some identify stimuli either in terms of the physical activation of the sensory organs or in terms of the behavioral response they are associated with, other researchers opt for defining stimuli in objective physical terms. We find important differences even within those who relate stimuli to behavior. For instance, whereas some behaviorists are interested in physical responses (e.g., muscle contraction) to identify stimuli, others, like Tolman and Holt, are interested in what the organism is purposefully responding to. Moreover, there is confusion about whether stimuli exist in the world or only at the receptors, and whether stimuli, being discrete and atomistic, can form structures. According to James Gibson (1960), these confusions show that "there is a weak link in the chain of reasoning by which we explain experience and behavior, namely, our concept of stimulus" (p. 694).

The theoretical critique concerns the implications the notion of stimulus has for the scientific explanation of perception. One thing all psychologists agree upon is that the same sensory input (i.e., the same state at the observer's sensory receptors) can have different causes. When a three-dimensional physical space is projected onto a two-dimensional surface, some information (mostly information about depth) is necessarily lost. Because of this, a large but distant tree can yield the same retinal image as a small but nearby tree (Figure 2). This issue is usually described by saying that stimuli are "impoverished" or that they are ambiguous regarding their causal origin. Because stimuli are impoverished, any theory of perception that starts with sensory stimulation must answer the question about how to disambiguate them. As William James had already identified, the most popular solution to this problem assumes that the brain combines sensory data with some prior knowledge to infer its most likely cause. However, this inferential approach creates another, even more pressing issue: we must explain how the **perceptual system** acquired the knowledge required for perception in the first place (Warren, 2021). This is known as "the problem of prior knowledge" (aka "the problem of the nonrepayable loans of intelligence"; see Turvey, 2019).

In the context of the ecological approach, this problem first appeared in a paper published in 1955, coauthored by James and Eleanor Gibson. The topic of the paper is perceptual learning. According to the inferential approach to perception, we progressively improve our capacity to perceive the world's properties as we gain new knowledge to "enrich" the received stimuli. The obvious shortcoming of this solution is that the knowledge necessary for perception cannot come from perception. This leaves us with two equally unsatisfactory options: either the knowledge is innate, or it is acquired in some extra-perceptual manner.

To get out of this quagmire, James and Eleanor Gibson rejected the original assumption: that perception begins with ambiguous sensory data. Instead, they introduced a crucial distinction between stimulus and stimulus information (or information, *simpliciter*), and advanced a theory of perception in which the standard conception of stimuli played no significant role. Such is the origin of the notion of ecological information.

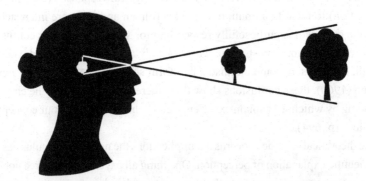

Figure 2 Depiction of the ambiguity of a retinal image. A large but distant tree creates the same retinal image as a small but nearby tree.

Let us unpack this idea by focusing on visual perception. The ecological approach begins by noting a distinction between radiant and ambient light. Radiant light is the light that emanates from a source (the sun, a light bulb, etc.). Ambient light, in contrast, refers to the light as it scatters in a medium. As the light propagates in the air, it interacts with the objects that furnish the environment, creating multiple reflections and reverberations. Because of this interaction, the ambient light gets structured, revealing differences in intensity and textures (shadows, colors, etc.) (Figure 3). This structure is what James Gibson calls "an ambient optic array." As opposed to the light energy that stimulates the retina, the patterns in the ambient optic array – sometimes called "higher-order variables of stimulation" in contrast with "lower-order variables" such as wavelength or amplitude – are the ones that provide information for the visual perception of the environment.

> For an information-based theory of perception that purports to replace sensation-based theories of perception the distinction between *stimulation* and *information* is crucial. . . . The conception of a structured *array* of ambient light (or an array of contacts, vibrations, or substances), is entirely different from the notion of stimuli that impinge on receptors. . . . It is perfectly legitimate to apply physical stimulation to an animal or an observer to see what he does or says, but one should not expect to learn about perception or behavior this way. For the latter purpose the experimenter must provide or display information. The fact that he must *stimulate* the retina (or the skin or the cochlea) in order to do so is incidental. (J. J. Gibson, 1972[1982], pp. 348–349, emphasis in the original)

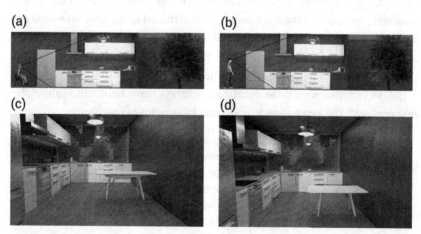

Figure 3 Representation of the ambient optic array from an illuminated kitchen. Images (a) and (b) represent the ambient optic array from a third-person perspective, including the change in perspective brought forth by agents when they occupy different points of view. Images (c) and (d) depict the same changes in perspective from a first-person point of view.

To make the difference between stimulus and information clearer, James Gibson (1979[2015]) asks us to think about a limiting (and somewhat simplified) case in which the air in the room is filled with a dense fog that impedes the light from bouncing off from the objects' surfaces (p. 46). In this scenario, the ambient light would be homogeneously distributed (unstructured), and there would be no differences to be picked up. Although there is light that impinges on and stimulates the visual receptors, nothing about the environment can be perceived.[3] Carello and Turvey (2019) compare this hypothetical situation with an experimental setting consisting of an empty box with its interior surfaces covered by a light-absorbing material, a light source located at one end, and a viewing aperture. If the observers are precluded from looking directly at the light source, nothing is seen, and they report no feeling of illumination. Light alone is not enough to see because information lies in its structure.[4]

Among the most important informational variables we can find are the so-called **invariants**. Invariants are patterns in the **ambient energy arrays** that remain unchanged under transformations. Invariants are crucial for the perception of environmental constancies. An intuitive example of an invariant is the "horizon ratio" (Sedgwick, 2001; Warren, 2019). Consider a series of telephone poles located at different relative distances. A useful trick to know whether the poles are of the same height is to observe the ratio at which the line of the horizon intersects them. Note that whereas the absolute height at which the horizon cuts across each pole will change, the ratio will not (Figure 4). Because the line of the horizon intersects objects of the same height at the same ratio (say 2:3), the horizon ratio constitutes an invariant for size constancy. Note that whereas some invariants are immediately available in the structure of the ambient light (or the sound waves, etc.), others need to be made available by the agent. This makes exploration a central element of perception (see Section 2.3).

But, in virtue of what do ambient energy arrays carry information about the environment? The key notion to understand this point is **specificity**:

> *[I]nformation about* something means only *specificity to* something. Hence, when we say that information is conveyed by light, odor, or mechanical energy, we do not mean that the source is literally conveyed as a copy or a replica. The sound of a bell is not the bell and the odor of the cheese is not cheese. Similarly, the perspective projection of the faces of an object (by the reverberating flux of reflected light in a medium) is not the object itself.

---

[3] Gibson reinforces this point when he discusses his own experiments on the *Ganzfeld* (J. J. Gibson, 1979[2015], p. 143; J. J. Gibson & Waddell, 1952). This is a homogeneous field in which illumination is not structured. In this situation, the observers do not perceive the surface before them.

[4] Note that the opposite is also true: we can have perception in the absence of stimulation. This is exemplified by the occluding edge (see J. J. Gibson, 1979[2015], chapter 11; Heft, 2019).

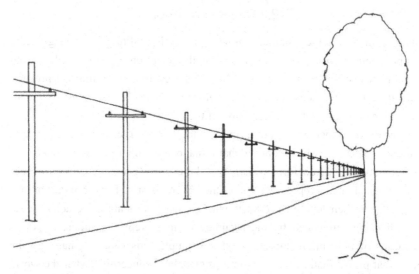

Figure 4 Representation of the horizon ratio invariant (Source: J. J. Gibson, 1979[2015], p. 158, figure 9.6. Reprinted with permission of Taylor & Francis Group, LLC).

> Nevertheless, in all these cases a property of the stimulus is univocally related to a property of the object by virtue of physical laws. This is what I mean by the conveying of environmental information. (J. J. Gibson, 1966, p. 187).

Coming back to the previous example, we see that the ambient light gets structured after it has been modified by the environment. This modification is not random or stochastic but obeys deterministic laws depending on certain properties, such as the geometrical structure or layout of the environment, the chemical composition of the objects' surfaces, the characteristics of the medium (air, water, etc.), and so on. Thanks to these laws, the structure of the ambient optic array becomes specific – that is, univocally related – to the structure of the environment. This means that "there is *only one* situation that could produce this distribution of light and *only one* distribution of light that could have been produced *by* this situation" (Blau & Wagman, 2023, p. 38, emphasis original). Therefore, the presence of certain pattern in the ambient optic array guarantees the presence of a particular property of the world that caused it.

This leads us to what Warren (2021) has called the "information hypothesis" in ecological psychology: "For every perceivable property of the environment, however subtle, there must be a higher order variable of information, however complex, that specifies it" (p. 2). The goal of ecological psychologists is hence to find the information variables that make it possible that organisms success-fully perceive particular properties of the environment.

2.2 Direct Perception

The hypothesis of the specificity of perceptual information carries a significant implication. If we reject it and assume that perception originates solely from ambiguous sensory data, we are led to see perception as an indirect process, mediated by inferences and prior knowledge, ultimately resulting in the construction of an internal representation of the external world.

The theory of perception put forth by Marr (1982) serves as a prime example of this perspective. Marr proposed that visual perception involves a sequence of computations that transform initially two-dimensional retinal images into three-dimensional mental representations of the external world. These representations can vary in their level of accuracy, with the observer's ability to adapt to the world being influenced by the accuracy of these representations. Bayesian theories of perception provide another example, this time emphasizing the role that probabilistic inferences and prior beliefs concerning what the world is like play in perception (Clark, 2016; Hohwy, 2013).

In contrast, ecological psychologists accept the hypothesis of the specificity of perceptual information and think that perception is direct. This means that individuals can be aware of certain properties of the environment without the need for mediating knowledge-based inferences. According to the idea of specificity, the presence of a particular property or event, α, in the environment lawfully generates a distinct pattern, β, in the energy array, given some **ecological constraints**.[5] Consequently, the ocurrence of β guarantees the presence of α. Specificity thus marks the difference between an informational variable and a mere probabilistic cue.

Since perceptual inferences were introduced to explain how individuals perceive the environment when all that they have are ambiguous stimuli, a theory that does not rely on this assumption can eliminate the need for perceptual inferences. Said differently, perceptual inferences are of no

---

[5] Ecological constraints are the physical laws and other reliable regularities within which species (and their perceptual systems) have evolved. Structural patterns of ambient energy arrays are informative within the ecological constraints of a species' niche. For instance, the intensity of light declines as the distance from the source increases at a rate described by the Inverse Square Law. This and other laws (e.g., electromagnetism) set the conditions for texture gradients to specify and inform about properties or events in the environment. Likewise, gravity causes terrestrial animals and objects to rest on the ground, thus making the horizon ratio informative about relative size. Importantly, individuals do not need to have prior knowledge of these physical laws to perceive the world. They only need to attune to the lawful (specific) correspondences they give rise to: "Rather than internally representing external constraints, I would suggest we leave them in the environment where they belong. This would enable us to understand the visual system as *adapting to* the information they make available, in the course of evolution, development, and learning. The visual system need not internally represent facts about gravity or surface texture to enable successful perceiving, its neural networks just have to be tuned to the resulting patterns of stimulation" (Warren, 2021, p. 21, emphasis in the original).

explanatory use if the information available for perception is rich and unambiguous. Ecological psychologists reject the view that perception is a matter of interpreting ambiguous cues, and hold, instead, that it is a matter of detecting (or "picking up") specific patterns of information that exist in the ambient array. The main idea behind the ecological approach to perception is thus as follows: if β guarantees the presence of α, paying attention to β suffices to know about α. Hence, for ecological psychologists: "Perception is not the process of inferring a meaningful environment from meaningless stimulation. Rather, it is an ongoing process of detecting meaningful information that yields meaningful experience" (Thomas et al., 2019, p. 238). It is important to emphasize, however, that we do not perceive information. Instead, by detecting information in ambient arrays we perceive the properties of the world that gave rise to and are specific to this information.

2.3 The Theory of Perceptual Systems: Perception is an Embodied Process

Although James Gibson (1966) put much emphasis on describing the structure of the ambient arrays, he was explicit that this structure contains information only in a potential sense. To complete the story, we must enter the observer. The notion of the observer is nonetheless used in an ambiguous way in the theory, allowing for a dual interpretation (Baggs & Chemero, 2019; Segundo-Ortin et al., 2019).

The first interpretation identifies the observer with a particular species. Because different species have evolved specialized perceptual organs, what constitutes information for a species might not be so for another (Warren, 2021). For instance, whereas some animals are able to electrolocate, alterations in the voltage patterns of the electric field provide no information for human beings. Under this first interpretation, a structured pattern in the ambient energy can only be meaningfully described as information in relation to a particular species.

The second interpretation identifies the observer with the individual and refers to the possibility that they occupy a position or point of view within the ambient energy arrays (see Figure 3). When this happens, the observer can have access to some aspects of the environment, those that are specified by the informational variables available for a static, motionless perspective. This motionless observer is a limiting case, though. On the contrary, natural observers move and look around, and this movement is essential for perception. Recall that a static image of a small but nearby tree becomes indistinguishable from a large, but distant tree. These two situations are impossible to discern from a static point of view, but not so for a moving observer. For instance, if we move to generate visual parallax, we can see that the speeds at which the trees change position in our visual field are different. Because the different speeds at which the trees "move" is lawfully related to their relative distance to the observer, they provide unambiguous information for the perception of depth. The relevance of exploration for perception is even clearer in the domain of haptic perception, where observers can only perceive certain properties of objects (their rigidity, their length, their mass, etc.) after manipulating them. By acting in an environment, we can generate new information that is specific to it.

James Gibson (1979[2015]) was very critical of a great part of perceptual science precisely because it disregarded the role of exploration in perception. He claims that as soon as we note that natural perception involves moving, scanning, and the like, we must conclude that "most of the experiments by psychologists, including the gestalt psychologists, have been irrelevant" (p. 257). In other words, we have been fooled into believing that we can yield valuable knowledge about perception from experiments where observers are forced to stay still while looking at drawings from the distance, or to glimpse inside a room through a narrow peephole. In contrast, natural perception involves movement and exploration.

Three implications follow from taking seriously the role of the individual in perception. First, whenever the agent occupies a point of view, the light that bounces off the objects' surfaces does not only contain information about the objects but about the perceiver too (e.g., her height), and about the relation between the perceiver and the environment (e.g., the relative distance between her and the objects). Likewise, when the observer moves toward a surface, they can observe that texture elements radiate out from the center of the visual field – a phenomenon called "optic looming" or "optical expansion." This expansion contains information about the observer's movement (i.e., its direction), and about the temporal gap remaining until making physical contact with the object. For James Gibson (1979[2015], chapter 7), this implies that self-perception accompanies exteroception like two sides of the same coin, and that to perceive the environment is to coperceive oneself.

The second implication is a radically new notion of perception, according to which perception is something we *do*, instead of something that merely happens as our receptors get stimulated. James Gibson captures this idea quite poetically when he writes that "[p]erceiving is an achievement of the individual, not an appearance in the theatre of his consciousness" (J. J. Gibson, 1979[2015], p. 228). The reason for this is two-fold. First, we have insisted that perception does not reduce to sensory stimulation. Rather, perception requires that the observer detects or "picks up" the specifying informational variables. For this, the observer must scan the ambient energy array, focusing their attention on these variables. Second, the required informational variables are not always given, but need to be generated by the observer's own movement. This entails an approach to perception in which the analysis of sensory inputs is replaced "with the analysis of the activities of feeling, tasting, smelling, listening, and looking" (Reed & Jones, 1982, p. 287). Unlike stimuli, information is obtained by the agent and not passively imposed, and perception is a skill at which we can improve (E. J. Gibson, 1969; E. J. Gibson & Pick, 2000).

The third implication is the idea of perceptual systems. Whereas perceptual psychologists have been interested in studying sensory receptors only, James and Eleanor Gibson describe perception as an embodied process. For instance, speaking of visual perception, James Gibson (1979[2015] writes: "one sees the environment not with the eyes but with the eyes-in-the-head-on-the-body-resting-on-the-ground" (p. 195). This embodied character of perception is condensed in the idea of perceptual systems, to which he dedicated his second book (J. J. Gibson, 1966). Perceptual systems are compounds of organized bodily structures that are grouped together because they contribute to the detection of perceptual variables of some kind. Perceptual systems are thus functional units. The visual system, for instance, comprises the eyes, the optic nerve, and the brain; but also the muscles that make it possible to move the eyes and the head, as well as those that facilitate locomotion and object manipulation while maintaining postural equilibrium. Because all these components play a part in the detection of visual information, they all belong to the visual system. Beyond the visual system, the catalog of perceptual systems includes the basic orientation system, the auditory system, the haptic system, and the taste–smell systems, all spanning multiple bodily organs. It is worth noting that different perceptual systems can pick up the same informational variables, thus opening the possibility of substituting one with another in certain circumstances (see Lobo et al., 2014, Lobo et al., 2019). The idea of perceptual systems thus marks a crucial distinction with previous theories of perception:

> The standard approach never gets around to ambient vision with head turning, and it does not even consider ambulatory vision. The process of perception is supposed to be localized in the head, not in the muscles, and it begins after the sensory input reaches the visual projection area of the cerebral cortex. The mind is in the brain.
>
> The ecological approach to visual perception works from the opposite end. It begins with the flowing array of the observer who walks from one vista to another, moves around an object of interest, and can approach it for scrutiny, thus extracting the invariants that underlie the changing perspective structure and seeing the connections between hidden and unhidden surfaces. (J. J. Gibson, 1979[2015], p. 290)

Finally, the idea of perceptual systems also carries implications for physiology (Raja, 2019b). While traditional physiologists were concerned with how the activation of sensory receptors yielded simple sensations, James Gibson thought that the physiological activity of receptors was vicarious to the function of the perceptual systems to which they belong. Hence, if physiologists aim to contribute to an appropriate explanation of perception, they must study how the activity of sensory receptors, as part of larger perceptual systems, contributes to the detection of information, rather than the elicitation of sensations.

2.4 Affordances

So far, we have analyzed the idea that perception is an embodied activity, but perception contributes to action too. According to ecological psychologists, perceptual systems evolved primarily to facilitate that organisms adapt to their econiches, allowing for the choice of the right actions and the control of goal-directed behavior. This leads to the claim that individuals perceive affordances.

An affordance is an opportunity for action that an environment offers to an individual. Under a pragmatic understanding of meaning, affordances constitute what different environmental elements mean to perceivers. The ontological status of affordances is a matter of debate (see Heras-Escribano, 2019), and we have no space to make full justice to it in this essay. Instead, we want to highlight three properties of affordances that, in our view, are essential for their correct understanding.

First, affordances only make sense within the context of organism–environment systems. To illustrate this point, consider an ordinary object like a bottle. Whereas an average adult can easily grab and lift the bottle with one hand, a human baby lacks the necessary strength and appropriately sized hands to perform the same action. Hence, whereas the bottle affords being grasped to the first individual, it does not do so to the second. This is why James Gibson (1979[2015]) insists that affordances cut the objective-subjective dichotomy, helping us to see its inadequacy (p. 121). Instead, affordances entail a complementary relationship between an observer and the environment.

The empirical studies on affordance perception have been mounting since James Gibson first introduced the idea in 1966, and they support the mutualist perspective on affordances.[6] A landmark in this research is William Warren's experiments on bipedal stair climbing, published in 1984. Using a biomechanical model that scaled the height of the stairs to the length of the leg, Warren identified a critical point beyond which a stair becomes unclimbable. This critical point was

---

[6] For a detailed survey on the current state of the art, including human and nonhuman organisms, see Wagman (2019).

0.88, indicating that a stair is climbable as long as its height does not exceed 88% of the agent's leg length. Warren's aim was to investigate whether participants would accurately perceive the point at which the stair was no longer climbable, aligning with the predictions of the biomechanical model.

To study this, participants were grouped according to their height, and it was found that while the perception of "climbability" varied among individuals in absolute terms (with taller participants reporting the ability to step on higher stairs compared to shorter participants), the critical point of 0.88 remained invariant for all participants. This demonstrated that participants were capable of accurately perceiving "climbability." In addition to this initial experiment, Warren conducted two more studies in which he successfully predicted that participants would perceive a stair as the most efficient (requiring less effort) to climb when the ratio was 0.26. Subsequent investigations by Konczak et al. (1992) revealed age-related differences in the perception of this affordance.

Similarly, various studies have demonstrated that individuals accurately perceive the critical point at which a vertical aperture no longer affords passing through (Warren & Whang, 1987), and this perception has been shown to vary accurately in situations where the observer's body takes more space – for example, when in motion rather than standing still (Franchak et al., 2012), using a wheelchair (Stoffregen et al., 2009), carrying hand-held objects (Wagman & Taylor, 2005), and even during pregnancy (Franchak & Adolph, 2014).

Second, affordances are perceived directly, without the need to perceive the properties of objects and our own bodily features in order to infer what actions are feasible (Thomas et al., 2019). Ample evidence supports this view. For instance, Amazeen and Turvey (1996) investigated this idea in relation to the size–weight illusion. This illusion arises when individuals, presented with two objects of identical mass, mistakenly judge the one with smaller diameter to be the heaviest. The researchers constructed a series of objects known as "tensor objects," by combining two interconnected rods to form a plus sign, with an additional third rod attached perpendicularly at the intersection point of the preceding two. Furthermore, they strategically placed metal rings at various positions along the rods to create objects with distinct weight distributions. Objects with different weight distributions generate different forces when held and have different moments of inertia at the wrist – their resistance to being rotated in each direction is different. Moving the rods, the experimenters could create objects with equal mass and size, but with different moments of inertia, and they asked participants to wield them with and without seeing them. They found out that subjects' misperception about the objects' weight was not based on size perception, as it was previously assumed, but on their perception of objects' moveability (Shockley et al., 2004); they judged the objects to be heavier when they offered more resistance to be moved. This suggests that affordance perception takes precedence over the perception of other more basic properties.

Direct perception of affordances is made possible thanks to the specific relationship between the structured energy and the structuring environment. If the ambient light is unambiguous regarding the environment's properties, we can utilize it to control our actions. Hence, rather than engaging in complex computations to infer what the environment affords, we can become aware of these possibilities by detecting the structured patterns in the light that conveys relevant information. For instance, we can adjust the pressure on the brake pedal in a car by using a particular property of the optical expansion of the vehicle ahead to prevent a collision (Fajen, 2008), and even determine when braking is no longer possible and steering is required (Venkatraman et al., 2016) – more details on this in Section 3. The same particular property can be employed to intercept an approaching object (Cancar et al., 2013). All these studies provide compelling evidence that individuals are remarkably good at perceiving the action possibilities present in their environment.

Third, affordances are perceived within the context of larger goal-oriented perception–action cycles, with organisms striving to act adaptively in their ecological niche (Heft, 1989; Segundo-Ortin, 2020, 2022; Segundo-Ortin & Kalis, 2022). For example, a chair placed in the middle of a corridor will be perceived as an obstacle to avoid by someone who is walking through it. By contrast, a person seeking for a place to sit will see the chair (provided the chair is large enough) as affording this possibility. Individuals with different goals will attend to different informational variables from the chair, perceiving different affordances of it.

In summary, the theory of affordances posits a lawful relationship between perception and action within the context of an observer–environment system. As individuals explore their environment to accomplish tasks, they can acquire new information that specifies how subsequent actions should be controlled toward a particular goal (Figure 5). Hence, "[w]ith each step closer to the goal the information detected and used for action must become ever more specific, narrowing the possible action paths available for the movement system, until ultimately, at the moment of goal accomplishment, the emergent path becomes uniquely defined" (Araújo et al., 2006, p. 661). Specific information about affordances thus serves as the foundation of the ecological approach to perception–action, explaining how perception can effectively guide action without the need for internal computations.

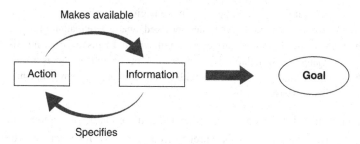

Figure 5 Representation of the interdependence of perception and action as proposed by ecological psychology. Perception–action cycles serve the purpose of maintaining the system's overall behavior in relation to accomplishing specific tasks or goals. By moving and exploring, the observer generates information that subsequently reveals additional opportunities for action. (Redrawn from Segundo-Ortin, 2019, p. 127, figure 6.1).

2.5 Perceptual Learning

We mentioned at the beginning of this section that the 1955 paper marks the division of labor between James and Eleanor Gibson (E. J. Gibson, 2001). Whereas James Gibson was concerned with formulating a general theory of perception and action, Eleanor investigated how perception develops through maturation and learning (E. J. Gibson, 1963, 1969, 2000; E. J. Gibson & Pick, 2000). Their projects, albeit distinct, are two sides of the same coin (Rader, 2018; Szokolszky, 2003).

The question that motivated the 1955 paper was whether perceptual learning should be considered a process of differentiation or enrichment (see E. J. Gibson & Pick, 2000, chapter 1). Far from being a trivial dispute, each position embodies radically different hypotheses. On the one hand, defenders of the idea that perceptual learning is a matter of enrichment take for granted that perception begins with ambiguous sensory stimulation, and propose that perception improves as we acquire new knowledge about the world and become able to make more sophisticated (unconscious) inferences. We have already pointed out that this assumption is predated by the problem of prior knowledge.

On the other hand, a differentiation theory assumes that there is specific, nonambiguous information in the environment from the onset, and that perception improves as individuals get better at finding and discriminating it. In this view, perceptual learning becomes a matter of detecting information variables not previously detected, and it entails an increasing ability to register relevant information from the ambient array:

> Perceptual learning goes on because in the beginning only gross imprecise information is obtained. Development proceeds via differentiation of information that specifies things and events in the world, by discovery of invariants as changes in stimulation are produced by movements of things and of the observer, and by encounters with novel and broader environments. (E. J. Gibson, 1991, pp. 288–289)

To flesh out this idea, Eleanor and James Gibson compared perceptual learning with wine tasting. To tell apart a claret from a burgundy, for instance, we must learn to detect the chemical signatures that specify their differences. In this sense, perceptual learning is a matter of discrimination, and it involves an improvement in our capacity to attune our perceptual capabilities to the higher-order variables of stimulation that matter for the tasks we aim to attain. Perception becomes less uncertain as individuals learn to detect more specific variables:

> [Perceptual learning] is a process of differentiation, the specification of significant information. It is, in the case of affordances, a result of selection from an array of information about the events, objects, and layout of the surrounding environment in relation to the readiness and state of the perceiver's own body structure and capabilities. (E. J. Gibson, 2000, p. 296)

To navigate our world successfully, we must be able to perceive what it affords. However, affordances are seldom perceived automatically – that is, direct perception does not mean automatic perception. On the contrary, we must learn to perceive them. This makes the study of perceptual learning an essential part of the ecological theory.

Perceptual learning so conceived is far from being simple. To begin with, it requires that we educate our attention so that we can differentiate and select the invariants that specify those environmental properties that are meaningful for what we aim to achieve (E. J. Gibson & Rader, 1979; Jacobs & Michaels, 2007; Segundo-Ortin & Heras-Escribano, 2021). The education of attention, however, is just one part of the process. Sometimes, the detection of invariants requires exploration, meaning that individuals must educate their attention while they acquire new ways to explore the environment (scanning, fixating, licking, whisking, etc.), generating new informational variables that lead to increasingly controlled performances. Finally, perceptual learning requires the growing and maturation of perceptual and motor systems, which implies that perceptual learning should be studied in the context of development too (Adolph, 2019; Adolph & Hoch, 2019; E. J. Gibson, 1994, p. 71). Development, including changes in animals' bodies, perceptual sensitivity, and the acquisition of new motor skills and action capabilities, allows for new possibilities for learning, expanding the perceptual world of the individuals. To this, we must add that the perceptual learning of human beings is often shaped by the cultural influence of their community (see Heft, 2018; Reed, 1996; Segundo-Ortin, 2022; Rietveld & Kiverstein, 2014).

Eleanor Gibson was very interested in developing a theory of perceptual learning that took into consideration what different species do in their ecological niches. Because of this, her approach was also a comparative approach. As Adolph and Kretch explain (2015, pp. 128–129), her idea was that we could formulate general principles of perception and development by studying the diversity of strategies that species use to know their environment. Her collaborative work on the "visual cliff" exemplifies this (E. J. Gibson & Walk, 1960). The experiment investigated the ability of human infants and newborn animals to perceive the possibility of falling from an apparent drop-off, thus refusing to crawl over it. Although all the species tested refused to crawl over the visual cliff, opting for the "shallow side" instead, later work suggests that for some species, for example, humans and cats, the ability to perceive these affordances requires previous locomotion experience (Kretch & Adolph, 2013).

In sum, the ecological approach conceives of perceptual learning as an increased ability to detect information about affordances, events, and other properties of the world. Exploratory activity is crucial to this process, as well as motor development and the maturation of perceptual systems. Whereas infants can perceive some elements of their environment from the onset, during life, their perceptual abilities grow, allowing them to discriminate more properties and reduce uncertainty about what is doable. Perceptual learning thus conduces to an increased correspondence between what is perceived and what the environment affords.

3 Ecological Psychology Today

In 1979, just before his death, James Gibson published *The ecological approach to visual perception.* It was perhaps his most successful book insofar as it presented the most developed theory of affordances up to date. This success was paradoxical, though. On the one hand, the concept of affordance grew beyond ecological psychology and now it is used in many different fields, from architecture to design, for instance (Djebbara, 2022; but see Segundo-Ortin & Heras-Escribano, 2023). In a way, affordances are the main contribution of James Gibson to human knowledge. On the other hand, he was already an eminent dissident of the cognitive sciences in 1979 (Costall & Morris, 2015). He stood against the computational-cum-representational theory of cognition that became mainstream during the 1960s and 1970s and, therefore, the ecological position remained (and still remains) minoritarian in the field.

Nevertheless, the works of James and Eleanor Gibson influenced an heterogenous group of scholars. Some of these scholars were already well established in psychology and the cognitive sciences. This is the case, for instance, of Ulrich Neisser (1967). After writing one of the early main works in cognitive science, *Cognitive psychology*, Neisser moved to Cornell and became a fellow of both James and Eleanor. A few years and many discussions later, Neisser (1976) became convinced that at least some aspects of the ecological approach were true, as it is reflected in his *Cognition and reality*.[7] Some other scholars influenced by James and Eleanor Gibson were students and early career researchers who ended up constructing ecological psychology as we understand it nowadays. Their joint efforts provided the ecological approach to perception and action with a growing theoretical and empirical corpus that began in the 1980s and is very well alive today.

3.1 Toward Ecological Psychology

James and Eleanor Gibson's decision of splitting labor had consequences in the configuration of ecological psychology in the years after James died. Whereas Eleanor and her students continued the pursuit of an ecological theory of perceptual development and learning, the building up of a general theory of perception and action from the ecological standpoint rested upon the shoulders of some early career researchers that were highly influenced by the works of James.

Among those following James Gibson's line of research in the early 1980s, a group of researchers based on what eventually would become the Center for the Ecological Study of Perception and Action (CESPA) at the University of Connecticut took a prominent role – see Turvey (2019). They were Claudia Carello, Carol Fowler, Claire Michaels, Robert Shaw, and Michael Turvey, among others. Along with other research groups, like the one led by David Lee at the University of Edinburgh (Scotland) and the one led by William Mace at Trinity College (USA), they were crucially involved in launching the scientific journal *Ecological Psychology*, initiating The International Society for Ecological Psychology, and promoting a biannual conference (the International Conference on Perception and Action). Moreover, they have educated most of the practicing ecological psychologists nowadays and had a crucial influence in the theoretical and methodological advances within the ecological approach. In terms of methodology, members of CESPA championed the use of **dynamical systems** theory and **nonlinear methods** in experimental psychology (see Section 3.2). Theoretically, they further worked out some of the

---

[7] Neisser said in some interviews (jokingly, we guess) that he used to wake up at night frightened and thinking "What if Jimmy is right?!" in reference to James Gibson.

main concepts of the ecological approach and embraced the explanatory strategy of modern physics to apply it to perception and action.

As noted in Section 2, one of the main theoretical contributions of the ecological approach to perception and action is taking the organism–environment system as the proper unit of analysis in psychology. Psychological functions must then be explained in a way that highlights the regularities at the organism–environment scale – that is, the **ecological scale**. This commitment entails not only searching for methods able to capture those regularities but also providing advances in their description and theoretical analysis. To do so, early Gibsonians sought to offer "a systematic explication" of one of "[James] Gibson's (2015) basic claims, namely, that there are *ecological laws relating organisms to the affordances of the environment*" (Turvey et al., 1981, p. 237; emphasis added).

The recourse to ecological laws makes the explanatory strategy of ecological psychologists akin to the one in modern physics. Instead of searching for neuro-psychological mechanisms to explain perception, they look for lawful relationships between some aspects of the environment and the perceptual states of the organism. In this context, perception and action follow ecological laws that apply to the whole organism–environment system as much as the mechanical laws of the solar system apply to the whole system. This does not mean or even entail that the solar system and the organism–environment system are the same. There are obvious differences between them like, for instance, that the organism–environment dynamics include a form of agency absent in the case of the solar system. What accounts for the resemblance between ecological psychology and modern physics is the common explanatory strategy and not the similarity of the objects of study.

An explanatory strategy modeled after modern physics was hardly a novelty in the history of experimental psychology. Kurt Lewin (1931) and E. B. Holt (1915b) had defended such a lawful approach, for instance. Due to these influences and his own convictions regarding scientific explanation, James Gibson was arguably also on board of an explanatory strategy based on the description of perceptual and behavioral laws in terms of organism–environment dynamics (see Raja, 2019a; Raja et al., 2017). In his biography of James Gibson, Edward Reed (1988) writes: "Like Einstein, [James] Gibson was willing to accept statistical models for lack of better descriptions of complex phenomena, but he believed that lawfully deterministic explanations should be forthcoming" (p. 207).

Despite this belief, James Gibson never pursued a formalization of the strategy. To do so, early ecological psychologists needed not only to find new mathematical methods, but also more concrete descriptions of what counts as ecological information and how organisms relate to affordances. If we take visual perception as the guiding example, the key was the further development and formalization of James Gibson's ecological optics. Three concepts received special attention: a new one, the *low-energy information medium*, and two that we have already talked about, *specification* and *invariants*.

Unlike the objects and surfaces of the environment, the medium (i.e., ambient light, vibrating air, chemicals, and so on) is in more or less continuous contact with the organism's perceptual systems. As such, it can influence their behavior. But, how so? Obviously, this influence is not based on forces – that is, neither depends on the mass of the medium arrays nor can it be described in purely mechanical terms. Rather, it is based on the geometry of the medium and the ways it changes as organisms move about. These geometrical properties are referred to as low-energy properties (i.e., mass-less properties), and their influence on organisms is understood in terms of information: "[I]nformation is implied whenever and wherever trajectories of a system are stable and reproducible in a field but are not the result of the field acting directly on the system through the mass dimension (conventionally, through forces). By this implication, the trajectories of [living and cognitive] systems are information-guided" (Kugler & Turvey, 1987, p. 9).

The sense in which the **low-energy medium** becomes informational has to do with its geometrical properties. As we have seen in Section 2, optical, acoustical, and chemical arrays are just structured patterns of light, air, and chemicals that emerge from the lawful relationships between the medium and other (high-energy) elements of the environment (e.g., the layout of potentials and reflective surfaces). The lawful structuring of the geometry of the energy array is what makes it specific and thus informational about it:

> The macroscopic, lawfully generated patterns envisaged by Gibson carry, in their topological form, properties that are specific to components of change and components of persistence in the living system-surround relation, and they are meaningful because they define gradient values with respect to the living system's internal potentials. The conceptual promise is that the information carried in the *evolving geometry of structured energy distributions* can be information *about* the living system's dynamics . . . relative to the environmental dynamics. (Kugler & Turvey, 1987, pp. 9–10; emphasis in the original)

With this conceptual promise came a new conceptualization of invariants which reflected the newly introduced terminology and allowed for its formalization. As organisms move around their environment, the geometry of the structured energy available to them is transformed in a way lawfully related to their own movement and other changes in their environment. An example of this is **optic flow** (Warren, 1998). Optic flow refers to the changes in the geometry of the structured light brought forth by the organism's own movements and other environmental events. Importantly, some aspects of this optic flow remain invariant with respect to some of these transformations. For instance, in the case of forward locomotion, the global optic flow exhibits a centrifugal pattern from the focus of expansion – that is, all the points of the visual field move away from its central point, which remains static. Similarly, in the case of backward locomotion, the global optic flow exhibits a centripetal pattern toward the focus of expansion – that is, all the points of the visual field collapse into its central point, which remains static. These two patterns, centrifugal and centripetal, are invariantly connected to forward and backward locomotion, respectively. Another example of an invariant property of the optical flow is the "horizon ratio" we have already referred to in the previous section.

However, as Claire Michaels and Claudia Carello (1981) noted, the patterns of global optic flow and the horizon ratio are not invariants of the same kind. On the one hand, we have "structural invariants." Structural invariants are those that "remain constant even though there are other properties that change" (Michaels & Carello, 1981, p. 25). An example of a structural invariant is a musical melody: the relationships between the different notes of the melody remains the same even when it is played in different keys. The horizon ratio is also a kind of structural invariant. The relationship

$$\text{Horizon Ratio} = B/A \tag{1},$$

where B is the part of the object over the horizon line, and A is the part of the object under the horizon line, remains stable while distance and shape change.

On the other hand, we have "transformational invariants." A transformational invariant is a pattern of change in "the proximal stimulus that specifies the change occurring to the [organism–environment system]" (Michaels & Carello, 1981, p. 26). Centrifugal and centripetal patterns of global optic flow are examples of this second kind of invariant.

The most famous transformational invariant is *tau* (τ) or time-to-contact (Lee, 2009). It was first described by David Lee in the 1970s and has since then being applied to a large variety of perceptual tasks both in psychology and neurophysiology. The best way to approach *tau* (τ) is to think of a ball looming toward you. As the ball gets closer to you, it expands in your visual field – that is, the closer the ball is, the more space it occludes in your visual field. τ is a property of this expansion. Concretely, **tau** is defined as

$$\tau = \frac{\theta}{\dot{\theta}}$$
(2),

where θ is the optical angle subtended by the looming object. Putting Equation (2) in words, τ is the inverse of the relative rate of dilatation of the optical angle θ subtended by a looming object (see Figure 6). It does not depend on the shape or any other quality of the approaching object, just on the change of the geometry of the optic array as it moves toward the perceiver. A simple mathematical derivation shows that τ is informative of "time-to-contact;" namely, of the time it will take the looming object to make contact with the perceiver if it keeps approaching at its current rate. Thus, τ can be used to control behavior in the context of timing a response – for example, dodging or hitting an approaching object, braking a car before collision, and so on.

Both the horizon ratio and **tau** (τ) are examples of variables of ecological information: well-defined properties of the evolving geometry of structured energy distributions. They are invariant and specify an aspect of the organism–environment dynamics. And they can be formalized as shown in Equations (1) and (2). Importantly, they can also be used to guide behavior. This virtue is crucial for ecological psychologists as their main aim is to develop a full-fledged theory of perception and action.

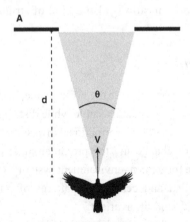

Figure 6 Example of **tau** (τ). When the bird is at a distance *d* of the aperture, the latter subtends an optic angle θ in the bird's visual field. As the bird approaches the aperture, θ expands. **Tau** (τ) is a property of that expansion. (From Fajen (2021), figure 7 (A). Reprinted with permission of Cambridge University Press).

Many early ecological psychologists, including Michael Turvey and David Lee, were highly influenced by the works of Russian physiologist Nikola Bernstein (1967). In particular, they followed Bernstein's idea that behavior is a coordinated activity in which the brain does not play an all-encompassing controlling role. On the contrary, behavior emerges from the complex network of relationships between physical, physiological, and ecological elements from which behavioral patterns emerge. James Gibson (1979[2015]) was himself sympathetic to this idea and he famously claimed "behavior is regular without being regulated" (p. 225). William Warren (2006) interprets this claim by stating that: "[R]ather than being localized in an internal (or external) structure, [behavioral] control is distributed over the organism–environment system ... [B]iology capitalizes on the regularities of the entire system as a means of ordering behavior" (p. 358). In this context, perception and action are characterized as self-organized processes constrained by a plethora of organism–environment factors, including ecological information.

The CESPA take on ecological psychology has been the guiding approach in the field until today and most empirical results have come from it. Additionally, its proponents have been responsible for the incorporation of dynamical systems theory and nonlinear methods into the toolbox of ecological psychology (see Sections 3.2 and 3.3). However, this way of understanding ecological psychology has not gone undisputed. Since the 1980s, the ecological approach has witnessed several discussions regarding some of its central concepts. Some of these discussions remain exclusively theoretical. For instance, there is an ongoing discussion on whether affordances are best understood as dispositions (Heras-Escribano, 2019; Turvey, 1992) or relations (Chemero, 2003; Stoffregen, 2003). Likewise, the explanatory strategy based on searching for ecological laws of perception has been challenged both within and without the ecological community, and notions of ecological information based on conventions or use have been proposed in the literature (Bruineberg et al., 2019; van Dijk et al., 2015; see Segundo-Ortin et al., 2019 for a critical reply) with the aim of better of capturing the sociocultural environment (more on this in Section 4.3).

A slightly different debate on the nature of ecological information, however, has been more relevant for the experimental program of ecological psychology: the debate on *specification*. The idea that perception is *always* based on the detection of specific information has been challenged on different grounds (Withagen & Chemero, 2009). The background of all these challenges is that behavior might also be controlled by using nonspecific information. Such a control strategy can be suboptimal in some cases, but still possible. The tradeoff between nonspecific and specific variables of ecological information has been central for the development of the experimental program of *direct learning*, for instance (Jacobs & Michaels, 2007). It has also been explored in terms of the development of babies and toddlers (see Section 3.3). In this context, the theoretical discussion on the specifying character of ecological information has been experimentally productive.

This is a good moment, as we talk about learning, to turn into the other main experimental framework in ecological psychology: the research program initiated by Eleanor Gibson and continued by her students and collaborators. These collaborators include Elizabeth Spelke, Cynthia Owsley, Arlene Walker, Anne Pick, Herbert Pick, Karen Adolph, and Marion Eppler, to name a few.

Eleanor got her hard-won, long-waited lab after James died (see E. J. Gibson, 2001, chapter 11). Her laboratory was built up to conduct research on perceptual learning in human infants following the principles of ecological psychology. This was clearly exemplified by her methods and theoretical assumptions (E. J. Gibson & Pick, 2000). For instance, instead of using geometric forms or pictures, Eleanor and her collaborators were interested in investigating the perception of real objects and their properties. Likewise, they were interested in multimodal perception, under the assumption that "[i]nformation for perception, from the start, is never confined in any event to a single modality, such as vision" (E. J. Gibson, 2001, p. 104). Following this view, some experiments were devised to study the correspondence of visual and haptic information for the perception of objects' rigidity and flexibility (E. J. Gibson & Walker, 1984). Another important topic of research was proprioceptive information, especially that which follows from the infants' own exploratory actions such as sucking, kicking, and the like. And, of course, perceptual learning in relation to affordances was a life-long interest for Eleanor: "The concept of affordance was the major theme of my husband's ecological theory of perception, and I wanted to study the way perception of affordances develops, for I am now convinced that what is learned in perceptual learning is the affordances of things, layout or whatever the infant encounters" (E. J. Gibson, 2001, p. 105).

In the last few decades, a major topic of research has been the interaction between perceptual learning and motor development (Adolph, 2019; Adolph & Hoch, 2019). This line of research involves the study of how changes in a perceiver's body – body weight, balance, posture, strength, coordination, and so on – brain, and motor skills, influence their ability to perceive and act on affordances. Crucially, instead of being the consequence of the maturation of prewired, biological programs, learning and development are understood as dynamical processes, leading to cascading effects that span the whole organism–environment system. Karen Adolph (2019), a graduate student of Eleanor Gibson, summarizes the research project as follows: "The general strategy is to identify an appropriate task, measure the affordance relations, determine whether infants perceive the affordances accurately, characterize the information-gathering behaviors that support infants' perception, and finally relate all of this to developmental changes in the infant-environment system" (p. 186).

This research is guided by some general principles which are worth mentioning (see Adolph, 2019). First, the central interest is on studying functional behavior – namely, behavior that serves adaptive purposes and allows perceivers to achieve their goals in realistic, ecologically valid settings (E. J. Gibson, 1982). Second, the emphasis is on understanding how development leads to changes in the infant–environment system. This brings two important implications. On the one hand, the view is that learning is "what an animal must do to cope with or exploit changing affordance relations" (Adolph, 2019, p. 182). Perceptual learning is necessitated by developmental changes, according to this view. On the other hand, the interest in flexibility (E. J. Gibson, 1994) is understood as the capacity to tailor prelearned perception–action loops to variations in local conditions. Finally, researchers give much importance to "real time," highlighting the necessity of determining the appropriate sampling intervals in which behavioral and developmental changes occur.

3.2 Dynamical Systems Theory and Nonlinear Methods

Ecological psychologists were the first ones to introduce *dynamical systems theory* (DST) for the study of behavior during the 1980s and, already in the 2000s, they generalized the use of nonlinear methods for the analysis of time series in experimental psychology. DST is a modeling tool that makes use of differential equations to capture the regularities of behavior given all the different factors that influence it – potentially including both ecological and physiological factors, as well as those that cut across the organism–environment boundary. In addition, nonlinear methods like $1/f$ scaling, recurrence quantification analysis (RQA), and detrended fluctuation analysis (DFA) can be used to explore nonlinear features of time series in order to unveil aspects of their temporal and structural organization which remain unaddressed when using standard statistical methods. The combination of these two sets of tools provides ecological psychologists with one of the most robust mathematical toolboxes in experimental psychology.

To understand why and how ecological psychologists use DST to model behavior, it is important to first distinguish between dynamical systems and DST. On the one hand, a dynamical system is just a system that changes in time. Under this definition, pretty much everything is a dynamical system:

an organism changes in time, the solar system changes in time, a computer changes in time, and so on. On the other hand, DST is a mathematical theory that can be used to study dynamical systems. DST provides the tools to define the changing variables of a system and the parameters and general rules that guide their change. The first tool is a language to talk about change. The second one is a mathematical formalism to make that language concise. Three key concepts of the DST language are **phase space**, **attractor**, and **symmetry breaking** (aka *phase transition*).[8] The phase space is the set of all possible states of one variable of a system. To illustrate it, we can image a landscape in which each location is one possible state of the system's variable of interest (see Figure 7). The change of the system can then be described as a trajectory through that landscape. The phase space is indeed defined by the variable of interest and a differential equation of the form:

$$\dot{x} = f(x) + \omega_i \tag{3}.$$

This kind of equation is called 'differential' because it describes the change – that is, the difference in time – of a variable x as a deterministic function of its own states, $f(x)$, and some noise ω_i. Let's say we are interested in how the traffic density of a city changes in time. Then, x will stand for a measurement of traffic density and $f(x)$ will describe the way x changes in time given some parameters, like the incidence of rush hours or the day of the week. In addition, there will be intrinsic variability of the process that will be characterized as noise, ω_i. The qualitative changes in traffic will therefore be successfully described by an equation of the form of (3) given the adequate variables, parameters, and rule. Moreover, if we take that equation and find its solutions for all the values of x, we obtain a landscape or *phase space* that encompasses all the possible states of the city's traffic density. As already noted, the actual states will thus be trajectories through that space.

The main properties of a phase space are its stable points. These points, also known as *attractors*, can be described as those states or sets of states that attract the trajectories of the system given some range of parametric values. In other words, they are the endpoints for the system's change given some parametric conditions.[9] For instance, the possible states of water if we take temperature as a parameter are gas, liquid, and ice. When water is heated up between 1 and 99

---

[8] We will keep DST definitions light. More precise definitions and their corresponding subtleties can be found in more formal introductions to DST (e.g., Strogatz, 1994).

[9] We describe attractors in a way the reader can conceptually grasp their significance. Attractors and their counterparts, repellers, are common but not universal. Some dynamical regimes, like the metastable ones, do not have stable points (Tognoli & Kelso, 2014).

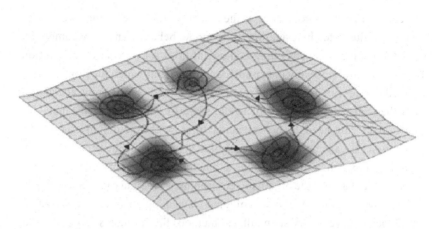

Figure 7 Hypothetical phase space/landscape. The dwells of the landscape are *attractors*; namely, end points of the state trajectories of the system (lines). Attractors can be points or set of points (spirals). The hills of the landscape are *repellers*; namely, points of the phase space the state trajectories of the system go away from. (From Hill, 2017, figure 2. Reproduced under a Creative Commons Attribution 4.0 License).

degrees Celsius, the attractor state is liquid. No matter what the initial state of water is, if it is heated up between those temperature values, it will eventually become liquid and will stop changing.

For some systems, however, the attractor is a set of states instead of just one single state. For example, the traffic density of a big city can show some daily stable patterns: rush hour early in the morning, less density in the early afternoon, another rush hour in the early evening, and so on. Instead of just one point of attraction, the phase space of this system would exhibit a set of points that follow each other in a constant cycle. In cases like this, the whole cycle between that set of states is considered the attractor – see, for example, the famous Lorentz attractor (Strogatz, 1994).

Finally, it is possible for the phase space to change its attractor landscape provided there are some particular changes in the parameters. For instance, if we change the temperature of water from 99 to 100 degrees Celsius, the "liquid" attractor will disappear from the phase space and the "gas" attractor will appear. In the case of traffic density, for example, a new law banishing all traffic in the city center might make the cycle-shaped attractor to disappear and a new attractor in the traffic density minima to appear. When the attractor landscape changes in this way, we say that the dynamical regime of the system has undergone a *symmetry breaking* or *phase transition*.

Ecological psychologists use these conceptual tools and the formal resources illustrated by Equation (3) to model behavior in a way compatible with the general aim of finding ecological laws for perception and action. DST does not impose any constraints on the scale at which the model can be applied; it does not matter if the relevant variable of the differential equation is at the scale of physiology or at the scale of ecology, for instance. The model does not need to be restricted to, say, the neural mechanism of perception. It can include that particular mechanism, but it can also take organism–environment regularities as the main explanatory elements, even when they cut across the organism–environment boundary (see Section 3.3).

The second set of tools that ecological psychologists have popularized in experimental psychology are nonlinear methods for the analysis of time series data (Riley & Van Orden, 2005). The starting point for the use of these methods is the acknowledgement of both the complexity of the organism–environment system and the complexity of behavior. As opposed to simple linear systems, complex systems encompass a great number of components interacting nonlinearly and exhibiting some global dynamics. Given this, we can expect those nonlinear interactions to influence the overall behavior of the system. However, such influence is not usually found in the final bit of a given behavioral outcome, but manifests itself in the temporal evolution of the behavioral process. To understand this, think of a carpenter hammering a nail. She hits the nail in virtually the same spot in every instance of hammering, but the trajectory of the arm-hand-hammer system is slightly different every time. The hitting spot repeats each time without repeating the same trajectory. This "repetition without repetition," this sweet spot between stability and variability, is a typical signature of complex behavior emerging from a complex system, and it can be measured when studying its time series.

Time series are just sets of data points temporally arranged. In the example of hammering, the time series can be a set of data points reflecting the position of the head of the hammer during the nailing movement, from the onset to the time in which the hammer hits the nail. Time series are common datasets when it comes to the study of behavior as they are a window to the way it is organized and controlled.

Ecological psychologists use nonlinear methos such as $1/f$ scaling, RQA, and DFA to explore properties of time series that are otherwise lost with more standard methods. The nonlinear interactions of the components of a complex system occur at many different spatiotemporal scales. Continuing with our example, hammering behavior emerges from a complex system, the activity of which spans through a variety of scales: from the microscopic interactions between neurons lasting just a few milliseconds, to the mesoscopic inter-actions between muscles and joints lasting fractions of seconds or longer, for instance. Van Orden et al. (2003) explored such multiscale character and proposed $1/f$ scaling as a way to measure the self-organization of intentional behavior. Put simply, Van Orden et al. (2003) proposed that intentions can be described as critical points – that is, points near to a symmetry breaking – of self-organized complex systems. In these critical points, so the story goes, the complexity of the system will be equally reflected at all its scales, effectively showing a fractal structure: the same patterns repeated in a scale-free fashion. Such a fractal organization can be measured in terms of $1/f$ or *pink* noise. Since the pioneering work of Van Orden et al. (2003), this kind of $1/f$ scaling analysis, or equivalent ones like DFA, have been applied to a wide variety of behaviors (Holden et al., 2013), including different kinds of social behav-iors in terms of *complexity matching* (Abney et al., 2014), that is, in terms of the coadjusting of the complexity of the behavior exhibited by the different agents participating in a social situation.

The other central feature of the nonlinear analysis of time series has to do with temporal dependencies. It is not only that complex systems can be studied at different scales, but their history is also relevant for their overall analysis. This is another reason why simple statistics that provide just a snapshot of the data are not usually adequate to study the emergence and control of behavior. Time series have trends, recursive moments, and so on, that inform about the overall features of behavior, and ecological psycholo-gists often use analyses like RQA to study them (Riley & Van Orden, 2005). RQA provides information about the structure of a times series, like its degree of recurrence and organization. This helps researchers to know, for example, what states of the system repeat in time or what are the different trends that can be found in a behavior. As in the case of $1/f$ scaling and DFA, RQA has been applied in a wide variety of ecological studies since it was first introduced. We now turn to these studies and some other outstanding results in the field of ecological psychology.

3.3 Five Decades of Experimental Results

The first experimental results from ecological psychology appeared in the 1970s. The use of DST started to be generalized in the late 1980s. And the use of nonlinear methods for the analysis of time series started to be common within the ecological approach in the early 2000s. This means that ecological psychology has been consistently delivering results during the last 50 years. It is, of course, not that easy to condense five decades of experimental work in a few pages, but we will attempt to at least provide a general view of the most important directions of research in the field. To do so, and in a markedly ecological spirit, we begin with perception and ecological information.

We have already introduced *tau* (τ) as a paradigmatic example of ecological information. τ is information about the time it takes for an object to make contact with a perceiver or, more generally, the time it will take for a gap to be fully closed insofar as its current closing rate remains stable. This gap can indeed be any gap between two arbitrary objects or processes. In this sense, although τ was first described as an optical variable of ecological information, nowadays it is regarded as a multimodal variable which may be present in many different energy arrays (Lee, 2009). Additionally, there is a wide variety of situations that can be described in terms of closing gaps: catching a ball (hand–ball gap), each step while walking (foot–ground gap), braking a car (car–red light gap), a neuron's action potential (min. potential–max. potential gap), and so on. These two considerations have helped ecological psychologists apply *tau* (τ) to an impressive variety of situations, like the plummeting of gannets (Lee & Reddish, 1981), long jump (Lee et al., 1982), the suckling activity of newborns (Craig & Lee, 1999), several musical activities (Craig et al., 2005; Schögler et al., 2008), or guiding the swing while playing golf (Craig et al., 2000), among others (see Lee, 2009 for a review).

However, *tau* (τ) is not the only variable of ecological information out there. In terms of the haptic system, for example, a well-studied variable of ecological information is the **inertia tensor** (*I*) (Amazeen & Turvey, 1996). Imagine that you grab an object – say a metal rod, or a tennis racket – and turn and wield it in different directions. Depending on where you grabbed the object (by one end, by the middle, etc.), and its mass distribution, each movement will require applying different forces, all of them corresponding to different resistances to rotations. The complete set of resistances to rotations that an object has when grasped at a particular place (the rotation point) can be described by the inertia tensor (Figure 8). A tensor is a quantity that varies in multiple dimensions simultaneously. In this case, *I* encompasses "the simultaneous differences in resistance to rotation in different directions about a rotation point" (Blau & Wagman, 2023, p. 126), and is usually depicted as a 3 x 3 matrix of values. Several experiments, including the size–weight illusion mentioned in Section 2 (Shockley et al., 2004), suggest that the inertia tensor specifies affordances regarding the manipulation of objects. *I* is detected by means of the patterns of deformations in the bodily tissue (hand, wrist, forearm, shoulder, and so on) accompanying each movement.

For instance, Solomon and Turvey (1988) asked participants to hold rods of different lengths and wield them six times with their right hand. The participants

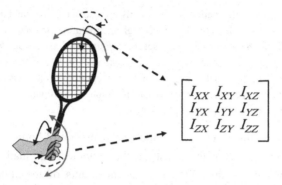

$$\begin{bmatrix} I_{XX} & I_{XY} & I_{XZ} \\ I_{YX} & I_{YY} & I_{YZ} \\ I_{ZX} & I_{ZY} & I_{ZZ} \end{bmatrix}$$

Figure 8 The inertia tensor of a tennis racket. The values along the diagonal are the different moments of inertia of the racket. From Blau & Wagman, 2023, figure 8.2. (Reprinted with permission of Taylor & Francis Group, LLC).

were sitting in a chair, and their right arm was hidden behind a curtain, so they could not see the rod. In addition, they were asked to adjust the distance between them and a visible marker so that the distance between them and the marker would be just reachable with the rod. Results suggest that the perceivers' capacity to estimate the length of the rod depends on their sensitivity to the rod's major principal moment of inertia (I_{xx}), corresponding to the object's resistance to rotating up and down. Following studies have investigated the perception of other properties (e.g., objects' shape, height, etc.), based on the detection of other values of I (see, Amazen & Turvey, 1996; Wagman et al., 2001). Furthermore, a series of experiments devised by Pagano and Turvey (1995) suggest that I provides information about the position of the limbs as well, this being crucial for proprioception (see also van de Lagenberg et al., 2007).

The inertia tensor is a good illustration of ecological information for a nonvisual sensory modality as well as of a kind of variable that is not as simple as ***tau*** (τ) or the horizon ratio. Variables of ecological information must be properties of the geometrical evolution of the energy arrays surrounding organisms, but these properties do not need to be simple. Indeed, the inertia tensor is a relatively high-order variable, as opposed to simpler ones like position, momentum, and so on. Many invariants are more similar to the inertia tensor than to ***tau*** (τ) or the horizon ratio. Among many possible examples (see Warren, 2021), the invariants that specify the edges between objects in the visual field are of the complex kind. To be aware of edges is important because it is crucial to differentiate between objects and to identify them as constant units even though their perspectival shape changes. Tsao and Tsao (2022) have recently provided a mathematical proof of the plausibility of ecological information for this task. Concretely, they use differential topology and prove that:

> [O]bject surface information is redundantly represented by the field of ambi-
> ent optic arrays through two of its topological structures: the pseudogroup of
> *stereo diffeomorphisms* and the set of *infinitesimal accretion borders*.
> Formulated in terms of ecological optics, vision is a fully constrained, well-
> posed problem. Complete information for perception of objects as discrete,
> persistent units is contained in the visual environment itself within the field of
> ambient optic arrays. (p. 3; emphasis is ours)

Stereo diffeomorphisms and the infinitesimal accretion of borders are the two invariants of the optic flow that constitute the ecological information for object segmentation and tracking. Similarly, the invariants of the optic flow that perceivers can use to control forward locomotion in natural terrains, flat or bumpy, are of relatively high order. Matthis et al. (2022) have shown *divergence* and *curl* to be invariant with respect to the transformations of the optical flow during free locomotion. These properties are, again, the ones that constitute ecological information as opposed to simpler properties of the optic flow, like velocity or bending.

There are other variables of ecological information, from chemical gradients (Kugler & Turvey, 1987) to the relative phase of different oscillators during rhythmical behavior (Bingham, 2004; Wilson & Bingham, 2008), but talking about locomotion is a good way to introduce the ecological modeling of behavior. Brett Fajen and William Warren (2003) proposed a dynamical model of forward locomotion in sparsely populated environments. It describes the trajectories of a walking agent given the constraints posited by the elements of their environment (obstacles and goals). Fajen and Warren (2003) model the goal as an attractor and the obstacles as repellers (see Figure 9). The model captures the changes in the steering of the walking agent with respect to goals and obstacles with the following equation:

$$\ddot{\phi} = -b_g(-\dot{\phi}) - k_g\beta_g\left(e^{-C1dg} + C2\right) + \sum k_o\beta_o e^{-C3|\beta o|}e^{-C4do} \qquad (4).$$

Equation (4) is of the same general form as Equation (3), where φ represents the steering of the agent, βg and βo are the angles defined by the agent, the goal, and the obstacles, respectively. The rest of the terms (k, b, and C_i) are parameters of the system. Equation (4) describes the changes in the steering of the agent as she locomotes by following two very simple heuristics: first, in order to reach the goal, the walking agent must close the βg angle; and second, in order to avoid obstacles, the agent must open the βo angle. This is why both terms have a different sign in the equation.

Fajen and Warren's (2003) model illustrates the way ecological psychologists aim to capture lawful regularities in behavior using DST. It is indeed a very

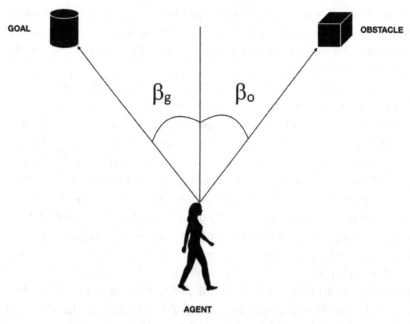

Figure 9 If we take the steering of the agent to constitute an arbitrary reference axis, such steering and the position of the goal form an angle βg. Similarly, the steering of the agent and the position of the obstacle form an angle βo. The goal acts as an attractor, and the obstacle as a repeller, both modeled by using the equation of a damped mass-spring represented in Equation (4).

robust model that has been generalized to other forms of locomotion, like haptic-based locomotion (Lobo et al., 2019) or group locomotion (Rio et al., 2018).

There are many other examples of the use of DST in ecological psychology. The most famous one is the Haken–Kelso–Bunz (HKB) model for coordinated rhythmical movement (Haken et al., 1985; Kelso, 1995). The HKB model has indeed been generalized beyond behavior and all the way to neuroscience in the form of *coordination dynamics* (Tognoli & Kelso, 2014). Other DST models in ecological psychology are used to explain learning (Newell et al., 2008), interpersonal coordination (Schmidt & Richardson, 2008), speech production (Port, 2003), brain–body coordination (Pillai & Jirsa, 2017), or behavioral variability (Nalepka et al., 2017, 2019), among others.

Beyond ecological information and DST modeling, ecological psychologists have pursued the experimental study of affordances. As Jeffrey Wagman (2019) explains, James Gibson's main claim was that "we go from surfaces to affordances when a point of observation in the optic array becomes occupied by a perceiver (with a given set of action capabilities)" (p. 131). This means that, even though perception is a process of information detection, we do not experience information but affordances: information detection yields the experience of affordances.

Consider again an everyday activity such as locomotion. One important factor in successful locomotion is to be able to identify those surfaces that afford standing. Regia-Corte and Wagman (2008) devised an experiment in which they asked participants to adjust the angle of inclination of a surface until they thought it was barely possible for them to stand on it while wearing a backpack-like apparatus with three configurations: high-mass, low-mass, and no-mass. Moreover, participants performed this task in two modalities: seeing the surface, and using a wooden dowel to explore it while blindfolded. Experimenters found that perception of standing correctly reflected changes in the center of mass brought by alterations in the backpack configuration, and that such perception remained similar for the two conditions. In both, perceiving the affordance for standing depends on the same variables, albeit explored by different perceptual systems.[10] Prior to that, Kinsella-Shaw and colleagues (1992) had already discovered that people are actually very good at perceiving the maximal slope a surface may have for them to walk on it. Importantly, individuals do so in relation to their action capabilities (Fajen, 2005).

Action capabilities are indeed fundamental for the perception of affordances. We have already mentioned that perceiving the possibility of passing through an aperture varies in situations where the observer's body takes more space (see Franchak et al., 2012; Stoffregen et al., 2009; Wagman & Taylor, 2005). But perception of affordances varies as a function of fatigue too. To investigate this, Pijpers, Oudejans, and Bakker (2007) asked participants to climb on a climbing wall in a series of trials, resulting in increased exertion. Furthermore, the participants were asked to judge their maximum reaching height before and during climbing. The researchers discovered that both the actual and perceived maximum reaching height declined when fatigue increased. Relatedly, Lee et al. (2012) investigated perception of target size by skilled and unskilled archers, with and without stabilizers. They asked participants to shoot at targets of different sizes but precluded them from knowing where the arrow landed. They found out that the archers' estimation of the size of the target depended on their perception of the "hittable-ness" of the target, which varied depending on how they coordinated their stance, draw, and aim.

---

[10] For other examples of sensory substitution in the perception of affordances, see Lobo et al. (2014, 2019).

Other studies have investigated how perception of affordances vary when individuals perform certain actions while holding objects or having them attached to their bodies. This is important because the use of objects while acting changes the action capabilities of individuals, which most likely affects their perception of affordances. Vauclin et al. (2023) published a systematic review of 71 articles studying this phenomenon, and concluded that individuals learn to detect new information about affordances that exist for the person-plus-object system only, and they recalibrate their perception to the action capabilities of said system. It is also worth noting that the research on affordance perception has also extended to nonhuman organisms (see Wagman et al., 2019 for a recent review).

Finally, ecological psychologists have also paid attention to learning and development. One important question within this line of research concerns the age at which infants begin to perceive and coordinate with relevant ecological information. For instance, various experiments have examined infants' ability to perceive *tau* (τ). One procedure consists of displaying videos of objects approaching the children and measuring when they blink. These experiments show that it is not until babies are around seven months old that they start blinking based on τ. Prior to reaching this developmental stage, infants base their blinking on absolute distance, which can result in delayed blinking if the object is approaching too fast (Kayed et al., 2008). Likewise, it has been discovered that babies about 40 weeks old coordinate with τ to achieve some lateral interception tasks (van der Meer et al., 1994; see also van der Meer & van der Weel, 2020).

Perceptual development has been studied using brain imaging techniques such as high-density electroencephalography (EEG) too. For instance, Agyei et al. 2015) compared the brain electrical activity of infants aged 3–4 months who were exposed to structured forward and reverse optic flow as well as nonstructured random visual motion, with the brain electrical activity of infants aged 11–12 months and with some experience of crawling. They report that only the children in the second cohort differentiate between both patterns of stimulation:

> With adequate neurobiological development and locomotor experience infants around 1 year of age rely, more so than when they were younger, on structured optic flow and show a more adult-like specialization for motion where faster oscillating cell assemblies have fewer but more specialized neurons, resulting in improved visual motion perception. (p. 436)

In addition to direction of motion, researchers have investigated how infants of different ages perceive motion speed (Vilhelmsen et al., 2019), occlusion, and the risk of collision (van der Meer et al., 2012; van der Weel & van der Meer, 2009). All these studies show important differences in brain activity, stemming from developmental changes and accompanying the acquisition of new perceptual-motor skills.

Another important question is whether the same information about affordances is exploited by individuals with different motor skills. For example, it's expected that with training and experience, infants learn to differentiate slopes that are too steep for crawling, preferring safer alternatives. The interesting thing, however, is that the same infants would attempt to walk down the same impossibly steep slopes they had learn to avoid if tested just after they have acquired the ability to walk. This suggests that previously acquired perceptual knowledge does not transfer from earlier to later skills (Adolph, 2019, p. 188). Because both tasks encompass different perceiver–environment relationships, with different limbs and coordination patterns involved, infants must relearn to perceive the relevant affordance in each case.

4 The Future of Ecological Psychology

We have now reviewed not only the history and development of ecological psychology with the works of James and Eleanor Gibson, but the posterior conceptual and methodological advances that made of it a lively scientific program up to this date. Ecological psychology is one of the main constituents of what has been named radical embodied cognitive science (Chemero, 2009) or 4E cognitive science (Newen et al., 2018). And new research paths have been recently opening and setting up the future of the ecological approach within a wider breadth of issues and topics.

The goal of this section is to explore some of the most important new paths and current developments in ecological psychology as well as their future prospects. We will focus, first, on the incipient ecological neuroscience. Then, we will address recent works on social coordination. Third, we will explore contemporary ecological takes on culture and normativity. And finally, we will turn to the ecological approach to skill learning and coaching, along with the ecological explorations of rehabilitation. Needless to say, there are other ecologically inspired research programs that we could not mention due to space constraints (see Blau & Wagman, 2023).

4.1 Ecological Neuroscience

Probably the most pervasive misunderstanding about the ecological approach to perception and action is the idea that ecological psychologists *do* not or *should* not care about the brain. The focus on the organism–environment system as the proper unit of analysis for psychology has been often mistaken for a rejection of the validity of all neurophysiological efforts to understand the role of the brain in perception, action, and cognition. This idea has been historically fed both from within and from without ecological psychology (e.g., Mace, 1977). However, it is not in the works of James and Eleanor Gibson and, as we see it, it completely mischaracterizes ecological psychology.

As we have seen, ecological psychologists take the organism–environment system to be a complex system, and behavior to be a complex event emerging from that system. Complex systems are understood as collections of many elements that exhibit a huge number of nonlinear interactions at many different spatiotemporal scales. Given this, there is no good reason to think that ecological psychologists *do* or *should* think perception, action, and cognition are explained exclusively at the ecological scale. On the contrary, if the appeal to complexity is taken seriously, a multiscale explanation, including the ecological scale but also the neural scale, seems to be more reasonable.

Most ecological psychologists are committed to the existence of ecological laws for perception and action along with specific perceptual information at the ecological scale. These two commitments entail that, whenever we want to explain perceptual experience and behavior, we need to pay attention to the regularities of the organism–environment system as a unified system. These regularities are not going to be found in a particular neurophysiological mechanism nor, for that matter, in the physiology of the arm or the fascia. However, this does not mean that we cannot study the contributions of the physiology of the arm or of the fascia to perception and action – indeed, ecological psychologists have already done so (see, e.g., Turvey & Fonseca, 2014; Schneider et al., 1989). And the same applies to neurophysiology: acknowledging the pertinence and centrality of the ecological scale does not mean turning a blind eye to neurophysiology. On the contrary, and at least for the sake of fully accounting for the complexity of behavior, it seems that the ecological approach would benefit from incorporating a story about the brain's contribution to perception and action as far as it is compatible with its central commitments.

Thankfully, the days of ecological psychology turning a blind eye to the neurosciences seem to be in the past and we are recently witnessing a growing interest in the possibility of an ecological neuroscience. Part of it has to do with the renaissance of DST methods in neuroscience (Favela, 2021). The use of DST in neuroscience, sometimes carried out by researchers friendly to the ecological approach (e.g., Pillai & Jirsa, 2017; Tognoli & Kelso, 2014), puts the study of the brain in the same language ecological psychologists employ to explain perception and action. This move alone has been enough for some ecological psychologists to find a renewed interest in neuroscience (e.g., Van Orden et al., 2012). The works of J. A. Scott Kelso and colleagues on *coordination dynamics* have been important in this regard too (see Tognoli et al., 2020).

For over three decades, ecological psychologists have taken the ideas underlying coordination dynamics as fundamental to understanding the organization
and control of behavior (e.g., Chemero, 2009; Kugler & Turvey, 1987). Thus,
applying the same ideas to the study of the brain is not that much of a leap.

Ecological psychology has also witnessed the recovery of James Gibson's
notion of *resonance* for its contemporary toolbox. Mainstream theories of
perception tend to use communication and computational metaphors to explain
the activity of the brain. According to James Gibson, once the main tenets of
ecological psychology are accepted, those metaphors can be changed:

> In the first case [communication/computational] metaphors are used, such as
> the filtering of nervous impulses or the switching of impulses from one path
> to another. In the second case the metaphors used can be terms such as
> *resonating*, *extracting*, *optimizing*, or *symmetricalizing* and such acts as
> orienting, exploring, investigating, or adjusting. (Gibson, 1979, p. 235;
> emphasis in the original)

But if resonance is a metaphor, to what extent can it be operationalized to do
some work within the ecological approach? Contrary to a widespread belief,
James Gibson talks quite a lot about resonance, especially in his 1966 book, and
provides a quasi-operational definition for it:

> [T]he available stimulation surrounding an organism has structure . . . and [this
> structure] depends on the sources in the outer environment. If the invariants of
> this structure can be registered by a perceptual system, the constants of neural
> input will correspond to the constants of stimulus energy, although the one will
> not copy the other. But then meaningful information can be said to exist inside
> the nervous system as well as outside. The brain is relieved of the necessity of
> constructing such information by *any* process . . . Instead of postulating that the
> brain constructs information from the input of a sensory nerve, we can suppose
> that the centers of the nervous system, including the brain, resonate to informa-
> tion. (Gibson, 1966, p. 267; emphasis in the original)

The most straightforward interpretation of this quote is that resonance implies that
ecological information is present both at the ecological and the neural scales. The
brain does not need to engage in a constructive process to enrich otherwise
meaningless inputs; rather, it just needs to be sensitive to the already meaningful
ecological information. This is the context in which James Gibson uses the "self-
tuning radio receiver" metaphor. Although sometimes misunderstood (e.g.,
Cutting, 1982), this metaphor is not that much about the brain *simpliciter* as it
is about the brain–information relationship. The brain is like a radio receiver in
the sense that it does not need to construct meaningful information from
a noninformative-enough signal. Radio receivers can be tuned to broadcasts
that already have *all* the information needed; all the voices, all the music, all

the qualities. Radio receivers do not need to include any words to what the locutor says nor any notes to the broadcasted melody. The signal has it all. Radio receivers must have all the proper systems in order to tune to radio stations and to sound (e.g., transducers, speakers). But none of these systems is in the business of constructing new information about the broadcast. According to James Gibson and his resonance metaphor, brains are the same: they are part of the perceptual system able to detect information, but they are not constructing information.

From this starting point, Vicente Raja (2018, 2019b, 2021; Raja & Anderson, 2019) has further operationalized the ecological notion of resonance. Echoing the view that ecological information is present both at the ecological and at the neural scales, Raja (2018, 2021) defines **ecological resonance** as the process by which the same perceptual information constraining organism–environment dynamics (O-E_D) also constraints neural dynamics (N_D; see Figure 10).

Raja's operationalization of ecological resonance entails several testable hypotheses. Some of them have to do with the relationship between the two scales at play. In a deeply ecological spirit, ecological resonance depicts the neural scale as constrained and nested within the organism–environment scale. In this sense, the neural scale gains its significance only as part of the organism–environment scale, that effectively acts as an enabling constraint for neural dynamics and that is fundamental for ecological neuroscience (Raja, 2021; Raja & Anderson, 2021). This is in line with the idea, proposed by van Orden et al. (2012), of the *blue-collar brain*: by virtue of their faster time scale, brain dynamics are controlled – in the sense of being constrained – by behavioral dynamics. Some preliminary results in this regard can be already found in the literature (e.g., Aguilera et al., 2013; see also Dotov, 2014).

Beyond considerations regarding the scalar relationships of the cognitive system, the most straightforward testable hypothesis that follows from ecological resonance is that, if a variable of ecological information constrains the O-E_D in a particular situation, the *same* variable of ecological information must constrain the N_D as well. For instance, if we describe a given behavior as *tau* (τ)-guided, we must find *tau* (τ) in neural dynamics too. This hypothesis has already been tested in a variety of situations and the experimental results seem to corroborate it. *Tau* (τ) has been found in the *nucleus rotundus* of pigeons (Sun & Frost, 1998; Wang & Frost, 1992), in the brain activity of primates while executing different tasks (Georgopoulos, 2007; Lee et al., 2001; Merchant & Georgopoulos, 2006; Merchant et al., 2004, 2003a, 2003b; Port et al., 2001), in babies' brains while performing a visual attention task (van der Weel & van der Meer, 2009), or in the brain of adult humans while executing interception tasks (van der Weel et al., 2022), time-to-collision tasks (Field & Wann, 2005), or just

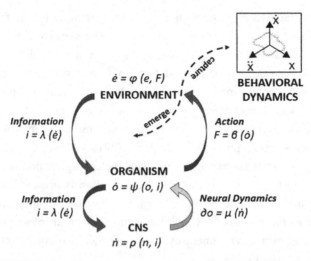

Figure 10 Model of ecological resonance. The top loop represents the dynamics of the organism–environment system (O-E$_D$). Behavioral dynamics (i.e., the dynamics of behavior) emerge from the organism–environment interaction, where the change in the environment is a function of environmental states e and the actions F of the organism. Information, i, is itself a function of e. The lower loop represents neural dynamics (N$_D$) and their contribution to the actions of the organism. As it does with O-E$_D$, relevant information, i, also constrains N$_D$ given a function $\rho(n, i)$. These dynamics constitute a proper part ∂o of the overall dynamics of the organism. (Source: Raja, 2021, figure 4).

simple laboratory tasks (Tan et al., 2009). It has also been used as part of artificial models of motor control (e.g., de Rugy et al., 2002).

Therefore, ecological resonance is starting to find some experimental backup, and has already started to permeate other theoretical approaches, like enactivism (Ryan & Gallagher, 2020) or computational neuroscience (Falandays et al., 2023). However, resonance is not the only concept from ecological psychology that has made its way into neuroscience. Affordances have also received a good deal of attention. Pioneering work on the neuroscience of affordances was developed by Paul Cisek and colleagues (Cisek, 2007; Pezzulo & Cisek, 2016). Since then, affordances have been neuro-scientifically explored in different ways, both theoretically and experimentally (e.g., Snow & Culham, 2022; de Wit et al., 2017).

Other researchers have proposed different ways to accommodate the tenets of ecological psychology within neuroscience. For instance, Michael Turvey and colleagues have tried to explore the role of the brain in perception–action activities in terms of thermodynamic benefits (Fultot et al., 2019). Jelle Bruineberg and Eric Rietveld (2019) have explored the compatibilities between ecological psychology and the free-energy principle (e.g., Ramstead et al., 2023; cf. Raja et al., 2021). In a different context, Hasson et al. (2020) have explored Gibsonian ideas in their proposal of *direct fit* algorithms for computational neuroscience and artificial intelligence. Overall, ecological neuroscience keeps growing as one of the main trends within ecological psychology.

4.2 Social Coordination

Environments are populated by many organisms. This makes social coordination an essential component of all species' cognitive repertoire, and ecological psychologists acknowledge it. According to the ecological hypothesis, social interaction, much like any other behavior, is also guided by the perception of specific information about affordances. This idea was already hinted by James Gibson (1979[2015]):

> The richest and most elaborate affordances of the environment are provided by other animals and, for us, other people. . . . Behavior affords behavior, and the whole subject matter of psychology and of the social sciences can be thought of as an elaboration of this basic fact. Sexual behavior, nurturing behavior, fighting behavior, cooperative behavior, economic behavior, political behavior – all depend on the perceiving of what another person or other persons afford, or sometimes on the misperceiving of it. (p. 127)

This paragraph suggests that there is a specific kind of "richer" affordances that depend on the presence of one or more interactive agents. Several factors contribute to this phenomenon (Segundo-Ortin & Satne, 2022). First, and unlike inanimate objects, other individuals act, transforming the environment and creating new information for perception. This creates the possibility of a social behavioral loop (Kono, 2009). Second, during our interaction with other individuals, they can either cooperate or resist, shaping the nature of the available affordances (Hodges & Baron, 2007). Lastly, social interactions frequently involve the adoption of diverse roles, thus transforming what affordances are relevant for us at different moments (Baron, 2007). All these aspects contribute to the complexity of the social environment and underscore the significance of perceptual learning to navigate it effectively.

Gunnar Johansson (1973), a prominent researcher of biological motion perception, collected the first evidence that we can perceive what others are intentionally doing by paying attention to patterns of information that specify those actions. To test this hypothesis, Johansson attached patches of glass-bead retroreflective tape ("reflex patches") to the main joints of an assistant dressed in dark clothes, and configured the setting so that the light hitting the patches was reflected to the camera, creating an extremely high contrast between the bright patches and the dark background. When the assistant moved, the motion of the patches was recorded, resulting in a video that shows a series of points moving. The first test consisted of a person walking along the studio, and all participants were able to identify a person walking after one or two steps. Following experiments involved other actions, like running in different directions, cycling, climbing, dancing in couples, or various types of gymnastic motions. In all these cases, "spontaneous and correct identification of the types of activity has been made without exception" (p. 204), which suggests that there is specific information about other people's activities that can be used to perceive what they are doing, allowing for social interaction and coordination.[11]

Leslie McArthur and Reuben Barron (1983) formulated the first attempt of an ecological theory of social perception in 1983. Following Johansson, their main hypothesis was that properties that are important for social cognition and interpersonal coordination, such as benevolence versus malevolence, in-group versus out-group, or gender and sexual receptivity, must be specified in "the stimulus information that people project" (p. 222). Importantly, they emphasized that social perception must be learned and trained as much as object perception, and they predicted both individual and culture-related differences.

Recently, Kerry Marsh and colleagues have developed what they called a "social synergistic approach" (Marsh et al., 2006, 2009). This approach combines ecological psychology and DST to explain how "social units of action" arise and develop, adapting to the environment to attain collective goals. A crucial idea of their approach is that an ecological study of social coordination requires that we take as the minimum unit of study the O-O-E (organism–organism–environment) system, instead of the O-E (organism–environment) system *simpliciter*. This perspective entails "that embedding an individual within an emergent social unit of action, a dyadic relationship or a group, provides new possibilities for perceiving and acting that both constraint and extend an individual's ways of interacting with the environment" (Marsh et al., 2009, p. 1217). Hence, instead of focusing on individuals and taking their perceptual-motor capabilities as the default explanatory mechanism to explain social coordination, the authors regard the temporary social unit as an irreducible, self-organized system.

In sum, the main ideas of this approach are: (i) that interpersonal coordination results from establishing interpersonal synergies – that is, "higher-order control systems formed by coupling movement system degrees of freedom of two (or

---

[11] Follow-up studies revealed that the perception of biomechanical invariant properties in a series of individual's gaits while walking suffice for the identification of their sex (Cutting, 1978).

more) actors" (Riley et al., 2011, p. 1); and (ii) that "the very same lawful processes that occur when an animal coordinates the movements of its limbs (intrapersonal coordination) also occur when two or more animals coordinate their movements with each other (interpersonal coordination)" (Blau & Wagman, 2023, p. 176). Consequently, rather than simply asking whether there is information from another individual that specifies some affordance, this approach studies the dynamics of the whole social unit, trying to determine, for instance, what sorts of tasks constraints and goals can create such social units, what aspects of the environment lawfully specify the possibility of creating a social synergy, and what sort of information specifies affordances at the level of the O-O-E system.

Richardson, Marsh, and Baron (2007) showed a series of wooden planks of different lengths to a group of people and asked them how they would grasp and lift planks. They give the participants three options: they could carry the planks with one hand, two hands, or with another person. What they found was equivalent to what Warren had reported back in 1984: whereas the decision of participants changed depending on maximum grasping width, they were all consistent with identical ratios of plank length to maximum grasping width (0.98). So, participants can perceive the critical value at which they need help from another person to achieve a goal.

Another key assumption of this approach is that the higher-order social unit exerts top-down causation over the individual participants. Therefore, not only does the social unit have unique capabilities distinct from the capabilities of the people involved, but the behavior and experience of the individuals change when they are part of the collective. Marsh et al. (2006) summarize their view as follows:

> [J]ust as perception and action are mutually and causally coupled to behavioral aims at the individual level ... the perception and action capabilities of the social unit are mutually constrained, ordered, and dynamically coupled in the satisfaction of a an emergent (dyadic) experiential (Csikszentmihalyi & Nakamura, 1999) goal ... Each individual's perception is coupled to his or her partner's action as it is to his or her own, and each individual's action alters their partner's perception just as it alters his or her own ... the perceiving and acting of those individuals within the social unit are causally entailed to form a distinct and irreducible system motivated by a mutually perceived goal. (p. 20)

To investigate how individuals' perception–action is altered in joint actions, Davis et al. (2010) studied how people choose to pass through an aperture together. In one experiment, participants were asked to pass through doorways of varying widths, both individually and with another person side-by-side.

The researchers observed the width at which participants began to turn their bodies in each condition (alone and together). As anticipated, the critical doorway width at which participants began to turn was wider in the side-by-side than in the solo condition. The interesting finding, however, was that the critical doorway width for the side-by-side condition was not the sum of the individual critical doorway widths: whereas in the solo condition individual participants turned their bodies when the aperture width was roughly 1.22 times their shoulder width, the critical point for the side-by-side condition was approximately 1.13 times the combined shoulder width of the participants. In other words, when passing together, individuals allowed less space compared to when they passed through the aperture individually. This discovery suggests that affordance perception in the context of social units is not an additive process.

The social synergistic approach has been applied to model and explain other instances of collective behavior, from simple situations such as two people coordinating when sitting side-by-side in rocking chairs (Richardson et al., 2007), to more complex situations such as group musical improvisation (Walton et al., 2015), or the decision-making of teams in sports (Araújo et al., 2006; Duarte et al., 2013; Travassos et al., 2012). Another interesting example is to be found in William Warren's models of collective motion and navigation in human crowds (see Warren, 2018). According to these works, an essential component of crowd behavior is a positive feedback mechanism in the form of a local neighborhood that gradually draws more individuals into the global motion pattern. This mechanism operates because each individual is perceptually coupled to and influenced by multiple neighbors and, in turn, influences others. This collective visual coupling is responsible for the propagation of the coherent motion throughout the crowd.

All these experiments support the view that the study of joint actions must take the emerging O-O-E system as the irreducible unit of analysis, focusing on the local interactions and global constraints within the system to explain group behavior as a self-organized phenomenon. This realization opens the way for a truly ecological theory of social perception and cognition.

4.3 Making Space for Culture and Normativity

One source of critiques against ecological psychology has been that it seems to obviate that human beings (and perhaps other species) are a cultural species, and that most likely their perception and action is interwoven with all sorts of cultural values and norms (see Hodges & Rączaszek-Leonardi, 2022). This may sound strange to some, considering James Gibson's early interest in social psychology (see J. J. Gibson, 1950b) and some of the examples he used to illustrate his notion of affordance (e.g., the mailbox in J. J. Gibson, 1979[2015], pp. 130–131). However, these criticisms are receiving a good deal of attention within the ecological community.

Alan Costall (1995, 2012) has been one of the most outspoken authors in this regard. Among other key contributions, Costall is famous for arguing that ecological psychology has not been able to make sense of the cultural and linguistic nature of human experience. According to him, James Gibson's continuing frustrations with cultural relativism led him to endorse a view of perception as fundamentally individualistic and asocial, and, with it, the view that "affordances are fixed and pre-existing, just waiting (from the beginning of time, as it were) for the appropriate animal to come their way" (Costall, 1995, p. 475). Against this view, Costall (2012) argues that many affordances, and especially those affordances that are most familiar to human beings, have a cultural and social origin, and can only be perceived by individuals with the right cultural background. He dubs these latter affordances as "canonical affordances." Costall has also problematized some crucial concepts of the ecological approach, including direct perception and specificity, precisely because, according to him, they do not square well with the social and cultural nature of human cognition.

Other authors have voiced similar concerns, though they did not go as far as Costall. For instance, Harry Heft (2017) claims that "it remains to be seen whether [ecological psychology] as articulated thus far can adequately capture the socio-cultural dimensions of human action and experience" (p. 124; see also Heras-Escribano, 2019, p. 176; Pedersen & Bang, 2016, p. 738). In a nutshell, the problem is that an ecological theory that focuses solely on analyzing how informational invariants shape perception might not be able to account for the impact that the sociocultural context has on how human beings perceive the world. Consider the following example from Heft (2003, pp. 157–158): while it is true that the invariant ratio between leg length and an object's height specifies the possibility of being climbed (Warren, 1984), this mathematical formulation falls short in explaining why we typically do not perceive our office chairs as climbable. Sociocultural norms determine what is appropriate to do in this (and other similar) situation, and that seems to affect what affordances we perceive at different times. Explaining this latter fact is essential to correctly account for human perception and action.

A promising strategy to face this challenge is to come back to the ecological approach to perceptual learning, but with a social twist. For instance, Reed (1996) has proposed a Vygotskian approach to perceptual learning, making room for explaining how others (e.g., caretakers) influence the learning trajectory of individuals by promoting specific affordances and shaping their "zone of proximal development" and creating a "field of promoted actions" (1993). Manuel Heras-Escribano (2019) has elaborated on Reed's proposal, bringing into the mix ideas from Dewey (1922[2007]), especially his rich notion of "habit," to suggest that normativity is first and foremost expressed in the individuals' tendencies to exploit some affordances instead of others. Similarly, Rietveld and Kiverstein (2014) have coined the notion of "skilled intentionality," arguing that by interacting with others, the attention of perceivers gets educated so that they are prone to perceive and exploit the affordances that are more appropriate for the situation they are in.[12]

Heft has contributed to this debate by arguing that perceptual learning occurs in the context of "behavior settings" (Heft, 2001, 2017, 2018, 2020; Heft et al., 2014). The notion of behavior setting stems from Roger Barker's "eco-behavioral science" (Barker, 1975, 1978) and refers to collective standing patterns of behavior that are intrinsically linked to specific community places – for example, churches, classrooms, and so on. According to this view, perceptual learning occurs when individuals participate in (or "inhabit") these behavior settings. Human perception and action thus get normatively shaped because they develop in places that are already saturated with a rich normative background.

Finally, Miguel Segundo-Ortin (2022; see also Brancazio & Segundo-Ortin, 2020; Segundo-Ortin & Kalis, 2022) have elaborated on a related notion, originally coined by Jacobs and Michaels (2007): education of intention. According to Segundo-Ortin, to fully account for the normative dimension of human perception and action we need to understand not only how attention is educated, but also intention. By participating in community practices and behavior settings, individuals learn what actions are permitted and expected from them, and with it, what affordances they should seek to perceive and exploit. This education of intention is manifested both in the perceptual habits of individuals and in their reflective practices, and it is part and parcel of the individual's perceptual learning.

In short, the challenge of how to make sense of the normative dimension of human perception and action is to explain "why some individuals, but not others, regularly perceive and exploit certain affordances in certain context, and why this is not exclusively dependent on their intrinsic properties" (Ayala, 2016, p. 882), without abandoning with the main tenets of the ecological theory.

---

[12] The so-called "skilled intentionality framework" includes a more relaxed notion of ecological information based on conventional rules and the idea that affordances invite or solicit actions (see Bruineberg et al., 2018; van Dijk & Kiverstein, 2020; Withagen et al., 2012, 2017; for a critical analysis of these ideas see: Brancazio & Segundo-Ortin, 2020; Heras-Escribano, 2019).

4.4 Skill Acquisition and Rehabilitation in Sports

Ecological dynamics is an applied research program that studies how expertise in sport is acquired (Araujo & Davids, 2011; Davids et al., 2008, 2013; Gray, 2021; Travassos et al., 2012; Woods et al., 2020). Its main aim is the production of successful training regimes for professional athletes, including the design of tasks and environments that improve rehabilitation.

Because athletes have different characteristics, including different access to affordances, and performing situations are never the same, defenders of ecological dynamics reject the view that skill acquisition is achieved through the repetition and fossilization of some prescribed ideal movement patterns (Gray, 2021; Segundo-Ortin & Heras-Escribano, 2021). Instead, they favor an approach according to which athletes become more skilled in a task by detecting relevant perceptual variables of ecological information and by exploiting them to constrain their behavior.

The relevance of ecological information in training and skill acquisition is well supported by ample evidence. For instance, whereas novices tend to pay attention to different information variables, including some which are not very useful for the task at hand, all athletes begin to converge on the variables that are more specific to the affordance they aim to exploit after the proper amount of practice (Pinder et al., 2011; Savelsbergh et al., 2002). This convergence toward the same information variables suggests that "the assembly of functional actions in skilled performance is a dynamical process dependent on relevant sources of perceptual information" (Davids et al., 2013, p. 24). Once the attention is optimally educated, the next step is calibration. Calibration is important because bodily dimensions and action capabilities vary, making it necessary that the athlete's perceptual-motor system be rescaled to the relevant information. Successful calibration results in actions that are appropriately scaled to the affordances of the environment and the current bodily capabilities of the athlete.

Degeneracy is also important in ecological dynamics. Degeneracy is a property by which structurally different systems achieve functionally similar solutions to complete a given task, and this is possible thanks to motor redundancy. For instance, it occurs when an athlete uses one motor strategy instead of another because the latter is no longer available or does not offer reliable solutions for the task at hand in particular contexts. In skill acquisition, "degeneracy" denotes "the stable yet flexible performance of skilled athletes" (Vauclin et al., 2023). Thus, in seeking expertise, athletes must exploit degeneracy, seeking new coordination solutions to the same problems and switching among them: using one and two hands to perform backhands in tennis, kicking the ball with the right and left foot in football, varying grips in judo, and so on.

Because degeneracy provides athletes with flexibility, robustness, and resistance to perturbations, an important goal for coaches and sport pedagogists is to help athletes explore and harness it. To achieve this, they are encouraged to design task-appropriate challenges that require the discovery of new solutions by the trainees.

Recently, Rob Gray (2021, chapters 7 and 8) has summarized two coaching methods compatible with ecological dynamics. According to him, both methods have the goals of disrupting the athlete's existing repertoire of stable solutions, promoting the exploration of the perceptual-motor landscape and increasing variability in movement execution and affordance perception. One is the constraint-led method. The main aim of this method is to promote perceptual and motor exploration by the athlete through the manipulation of task constraints. By changing the practicing situation, the coach can prevent the athlete from using a particular solution which is considered ineffective. One example is the practice of ball throwing with a connection ball to prevent the "forearm flyout," a common technical flaw in baseball pitchers.[13] Once the new constraint is introduced, the athlete is forced to find a new solution to achieve the goal – in this case, hit the catcher's target. Additionally, a coach can help an athlete explore more effectively by providing some "transition feedback." This feedback concerns whether the search for a new solution is heading in the correct direction. In the previous example, the transition feedback is provided by the trajectory of the connection ball. At the beginning, the connection ball tends to go to the side of the pitcher when it falls out; the pitcher is then asked to reconfigure her movement so that the ball goes forward when released. The changes in the direction of the connection ball provides the transition feedback for this task.

The second method is differential learning. As discussed earlier (see Section 3.2), all repeated movements come with some inherent variability. However, this inherent variability is not uniform across individuals. For instance, some tennis players display relatively minor differences in knee angle and racket–ball contact point from serve to serve compared to others. Coaches employing the differential learning method aim to introduce new variations into the athlete's movements on top of their inherent variability. In practice, this is accomplished by incorporating random fluctuations into the training environment – for example, adopting different body positions and body movements, introducing new perceptual information, and using varied equipment.

Ecological dynamics comes with its own challenges too. To begin with, psychologists and coaches interested in the acquisition of skills must adopt an

---

[13] For an example, watch the following video: https://www.youtube.com/watch?v=mSK7PnKm6Hg.

individual-based approach, trying to understand "how each individual learns to adapt their movement behaviours in complex and challenging environments in order to consistently achieve a particular task outcome" (Araujo & Davids, 2011, p. 8). One implication is that coaches should design realistic training environments that favor the perception and exploitation of some affordances over others, while leaving space for athletes to explore the "perceptual land-scape" and arrive at their own functional solutions:

> [P]racticing athletes need to be given the opportunities to search for and use information to guide their actions. This is best achieved through practice tasks that allow continuous movement interactions (not static drills), oppor-tunities for exploration of the performance environment (not prescriptions of a specific movement pattern to imitate), and inclusion of key information sources that will be present during performance (e.g., other players in team games ... and relevant court/pitch markings. (Davids et al., 2015, p. 131)

To sum up, successful skill acquisition is taken to be the opposite to the repetition of movement patterns through constant practice and the forming of an internal motor program comprised of invariant movements. There is no *one* way – the correct one – to swing a baseball, dribble a ball, serve, and so on, that we must train and repeat until we master it. Instead, defenders of ecological dynamics understand expertise as the athlete's capacity to adapt to a range of varying performance contexts, constantly renegotiating and reinventing themselves as key constraints change. Skill acquisition is thus understood as the "refinement of adaptation processes, achieved by perceiv-ing the key properties of the performance environment in the scale of an individual's body and action capabilities" (Araujo & Davids, 2011, p. 19). As the focus is not on movements themselves but on achieving a functional fit between the athlete and the performing environment, the designed prac-tice must include variations of the same perception–action task in different context situations, with the provision that all of them are relevant for the skill at issue. Finally, to ensure that skill learning is transferable, training regimes must be as similar as possible to the tasks the athlete would face in a real competition.

Principles of ecological dynamics are currently applied in training within different sports, including some top-level professional football clubs such as AIK Solna and Sevilla FC (see, e.g., Vaughan et al., 2021; Madruga-Parera et al., 2022). A different use of ecological dynamics is rehabilitation and injury prevention of sport practitioners (see, e.g., Crowther et al., 2016). For instance, prevention strategies for anterior cruciate ligament (ACL) injuries typically involve initiatives aimed at enhancing movement patterns that reduce biomechanical risk factors. According to Silva et al. (2019), these strategies can be roughly divided into three groups. One involves explicit instruction by the coach and promotes the athlete's internal focus of attention to their movements. The empirical research, however, has shown that even highly skilled athletes fare very poorly when trying to follow detailed instructions concerning how to change or correct their movements and technique (Giblin et al. 2015).

The second one is inspired by an information-processing, neurocentric cognitive paradigm and stresses action imitation along with external attention. Essentially, the athlete sees the contour of a model's body in a visual display and tries to imitate its movements, with the aid of visual feedback. The rationale behind this proposal comes from the discovery of the activity of mirror neurons: since the observation of a particular action activates the neural mechanisms involved in the production of the same action, action observation can be a good strategy to prime the neural circuits responsible for biomechanically efficient movement solutions. This approach, however, requires that trainees pay attention to many parameters at the same time, and it is "built on the assumption that biomechanically efficient movement solutions are embodied in neural mechanisms that can be 'awakened' and reinforced through action imitation" (Silva et al., 2019, p. 62).

Finally, Silva et al. (2019) advocate for an approach grounded in the ecological perspective: Augmented Neuromuscular Feedback (Kiefer et al., 2015). The basic idea is to provide athletes with implicit visual feedback about crucial biomechanical parameters. One way to do this is to couple the athlete's movements to easily visible figures in a visual display (a square, a rectangle, etc.) so that the movement of the athlete alters the properties of the shape in a nonarbitrary, specific fashion – for example, bending the sides of the square if the alignment of the knees and the hip is not optimal. Transforming complex movement patterns into simple visual feedback stimuli can provide efficient information for the trainee, avoiding the previously mentioned information overload. Once the trainee has learned the relationship between their own movements and the changes in the display figure, the instruction is to perform the task (e.g., jump, squat, and the like) to create and maintain the desired shapes: "Biomechanically efficient solutions naturally emerge if learners achieve the goal shape; if they do so repeatedly, over the course of practice through mechanisms of implicit learning, then the learners may develop robust movement patterns that protect them from injury when transfer to the performance environment occurs" (Silva et al., 2019, p. 63).

Although the Augmented Neuromuscular Feedback proposal needs more empirical support in what concerns its therapeutic application, there is ample evidence of the benefits of mapping movement variables onto simple visual feedback patterns for complex motor learning (see, e.g., Varoqui et al., 2011; Fernández & Bootsma, 2008). This evidence supports the view that a therapeutic approach based on ecological psychology is a possibility worth exploring.

Conclusion

We have tried to deliver an all-encompassing yet succinct presentation of ecological psychology, including its historical origins and development. As we have seen, the ecological approach begins with a radical reconceptualization of what it means to perceive. Whereas mainstream perceptual psychologists start with ambiguous sensory inputs that require to be enriched through unconscious psychological or neural processes, James and Eleanor Gibson propose ecological information as the foundation of perception. Ecological information refers to the evolution of the geometrical patterns of the ambient energy arrays that specify affordances and events in the environment. Thus, instead of taking perception as a constructive process, ecological psychologists think of it as an ongoing activity based on the detection (or pick up) of information. Ecological information allows ecological psychologists to get rid of internal processes to enrich otherwise ambiguous stimuli. Additionally, the active character of perception promotes a distinct approach to perceptual learning, focused on studying how perceivers become able to differentiate the useful information for the goals they aim to achieve, sometimes by means of careful exploration. This gives the study of motor development an especial role in the theory.

We have also tried to provide the readers with an overview of the state of the art in ecological psychology, including current interpretations of the most important ecological concepts and the methods that are used nowadays to study the dynamics of perception and action. We have also offered a review of the most important empirical results produced by the ecological approach in the last five decades. Finally, we have tried to show how the main tenets of ecological psychology are being applied to new realms of psychology and neuroscience, effectively expanding the ecological approach to the sciences of the brain, social and cultural psychology, and different fields of coaching and rehabilitation. We hope these efforts will be an invitation to current students and early researchers to learn and engage with ecological psychology in the years to come.

Glossary

Affordances: Opportunities for interaction that an environment offers to an organism. Affordances depend on the relationship between the organism's bodily features and abilities and the properties of the environment. Examples of affordances are the "climb-ability" of stairs or the "grab-ability" of a mug.

Ambient Energy Arrays: General name for the structured patters of light, air, chemicals, water, and so on, that surround different organisms at any moment of time. For instance, the structured light surrounding an organism is the *optic array* and the structured chemicals surrounding an organism is the *olfactory array*.

Attractor: State or set of states of the phase space of a system toward which the change of the systems evolves. Once the system reaches the attractor state, it stops changing.

Degeneracy: A property by which structurally different systems achieve functionally similar solutions to complete a given task. Degeneracy allows for flexibility in motor control as organisms can make use of a different system if a previously used one is unreliable or unavailable.

Direct Perception: Perceptual awareness of (at least some) properties of the environment by means of detecting rich ecological information. Perception is direct because it does not involve the inferential construction of an internal model of the environment through the enrichment of poorly informative stimulation.

Dynamical System: A system that changes in time. Dynamical systems can be mathematically studied using dynamical systems theory (DST).

Ecological Constraints: The physical laws and other reliable regularities within which species (and their perceptual systems) have evolved. Specific patterns in an ambient energy array are informative in the context of the ecological constraints of a species' niche.

Ecological Information: A structural feature of an ambient energy array (e.g., centrifugal expansion in the optic array) is described as ecological information when it bears a relation of specificity or univocal correspondence to some event or property of the environment to which it is lawfully related. Thanks to the relation of specificity between ecological information and the environment, organisms can be perceptually aware of the latter by detecting the former.

Ecological Resonance: The activity by which perceptual systems detect ecological information. Ecological resonance is relevant for ecological neuroscience because it predicts that the same ecological information that constrains the organism–environment dynamics must also constrain neural dynamics.

Ecological Scale: The scale of analysis that results from taking the organism–environment system as the main unit of study. According to ecological psychologists, psychological functions and events must be explained in a way that highlights the regularities found in the context of the organism–environment interactions.

Gestalt: German word for "form." It is used to refer to the formal/organizational properties of perceptual experience that cannot be explained in terms of simple sensations. For instance, a *group* of dots is a gestalt. We may have simple sensations for each individual dot, but we do not have sensations for the group as such. There are several gestalts and gestalt laws. The concept also gives its name to Gestalt psychology.

Inertia Tensor: The complete set of resistances to rotations that an object has when grasped at a particular place (the rotation point). The inertia tensor is usually depicted as a 3 x 3 matrix of values that change simultaneously with each rotation.

Invariant: Properties of the ambient energy arrays that remain unchanged under transformations. There are two main kinds of invariants: structural and transformational. Invariants are the typical variables of ecological information that specify properties of the environment.

Low-Energy Medium: Sometimes simply referred to as *medium*. It is the (semi)transparent element that surrounds different organisms and is almost constantly in contact with their sensory receptors. This medium is usually air in the case of terrestrial organisms and water in the case of aquatic organisms. It allows for arrays of light or chemicals, for instance, to be in contact with the sensory receptors of the organisms. The ecological hypothesis is that, when organisms move around, they can find ecological information available in those arrays. This way the medium becomes a *low-energy information medium*. The "low-energy" qualification has to do with the way such information influences the organism: not through forces but through geometrical structure.

Nonlinear Methods: Analytical and statistical methods to study the structure of time series at different temporal scales. They help finding elements of the variability of data (e.g., trends, scale-free properties, recurrence, etc.) that are missed in mainstream statistical analyses. Some examples of nonlinear methods are $1/f$ scaling, detrended fluctuation analysis (DFA), and recurrence quantification analysis (RQA).

Optic Flow: Changes in the structure of the ambient optic array brought forth by the movement of the agent or an event in the environment.

Perceptual Learning: The increasing ability of an individual to detect specific information variables not previously detected, thus improving their perception of the environment. This view is opposed to the conception of perceptual learning as a matter of internal, knowledge-led enrichment of impoverished stimuli.

Perceptual System: A compound of organized bodily structures that are grouped together because they contribute to the detection of perceptual information of some kind. One example is the visual system, which is composed by the eyes, the optic nerve, the brain, and all the muscles that make it possible that we explore the ambient optic array. Beyond the visual system, the catalog of perceptual systems includes the basic orientation system, the auditory system, the haptic system, and the taste–smell systems, all spanning multiple bodily organs.

Phase Space: An n-dimensional space that encompasses all the possible states of a dynamical system. It is usually represented as a 2- or 3-dimensional space encompassing all the geometrical properties of the system's change (e.g., the attractors).

Specificity: The lawful, univocal correspondence between some structural features of the ambient energy arrays (e.g., optic, acoustic, etc.) and the properties or events of the environment giving rise to them. The idea of specificity entails that there is only one property or event that could produce a particular pattern in a particular ambient energy array, and only one pattern in such an ambient energy array that could be produced by this property or event. It follows that the presence of this structural feature guarantees the presence of this property or event in the environment. Specificity marks the difference between an informational variable (in the ecological sense) and a mere probabilistic cue.

Symmetry Breaking: When the landscape of attractors of a phase space changes its geometry by changing the value of some parameters, we claim the system has undergone a symmetry breaking (or a *phase transition*, or a *bifurcation*).

Tau (τ): The inverse of the relative rate of dilatation of the optical angle θ subtended by a looming object. τ is informative of "time-to-contact;" namely, of the time it will take the looming object to make contact with the perceiver if it keeps approaching at its current rate.

References

Abney, D. H., Paxton, A., Dale. R., & Kello, C. T. (2014). Complexity matching in dyadic conversation. *Journal of Experimental Psychology: General, 143*(6), 2304–2315.

Adolph, K. E. (2019). An ecological approach to learning in (not and) development. *Human Development, 63*(3–4), 180–201. https://doi.org/10.1159/000503823.

Adolph, K. E., & Hoch, J. E. (2019). Motor development: Embodied, embedded, enculturated, and enabling. *Annual Review of Psychology, 70*(1), 141–164. https://doi.org/10.1146/annurev-psych-010418-102836.

Adolph, K. E., & Kretch, K. S. (2015). Gibson's theory of perceptual learning. *International Encyclopedia of the Social & Behavioral Sciences*. https://doi .org/10.1016/B978-0-08-097086-8.23096-1.

Aguilera, M., Bedia, M. G., Santos, B. A., & Barandiaran, X. E. (2013). The situated HKB model: How sensorimotor spatial coupling can alter oscillatory brain dynamics. *Frontiers in Computational Neuroscience, 7*, 117. http://doi .org/10.3389/fncom.2013.00117.

Agyei, S. B., Holth, M., van der Weel, F. R. (Ruud), & van der Meer, A. L. H. (2015). Longitudinal study of perception of structured optic flow and random visual motion in infants using high-density EEG. *Developmental Science, 18* (3), 436–451. https://doi.org/10.1111/desc.12221.

Amazeen, E. L., & Turvey, M. T. (1996). Weight perception and the haptic size-weight illusion are functions of the inertia tensor. *Journal of Experimental Psychology: Human Perception and Performance, 22*(1), 213–232.

Araújo, D., & Davids, K. (2011). What exactly is acquired during skill acquisition? *Journal of Consciousness Studies, 18*(3–4), 7–23.

Araújo, D., Davids, K., & Hristovski, R. (2006). The ecological dynamics of decision making in sport. *Psychology of Sport and Exercise, 7*(6), 653–676. https://doi.org/10.1016/j.psychsport.2006.07.002.

Ash, M. G. (1995). *Gestalt psychology in German culture, 1890–1967: Holism and the quest for objectivity*. Cambridge, UK: Cambridge University Press.

Ayala, S. (2016). Speech affordances: A structural take on how much we can do with our words. *European Journal of Philosophy, 24*(4), 879–891. https://doi .org/10.1111/ejop.12186.

Baggs, E., & Chemero, A. (2019). The third sense of environment. In J. Wagman & J. Blau (Eds.), *Perception as Information Detection* (pp. 5–20). New York: Routledge.

Barker, R. G. (1975). *Ecological psychology: Concepts and methods for studying the environment of human behavior.* San Francisco, CA: Stanford University Press.

Barker, R. G. (Ed.). (1978). *Habitats, environments, and human behavior: Studies in ecological psychology and eco-behavioral science from the Midwest Psychological Field Station, 1947–1972* (1st ed). New York: Jossey-Bass.

Baron, R. M. (2007). Situating coordination and cooperation between ecological and social psychology. *Ecological Psychology, 19*(2), 179–199. https://doi.org/10.1080/10407410701332106.

Bernstein, N. A. (1967). *The coordination and regulation of movements.* New York: Pergamon Press.

Bingham, G. P. (2004). A perceptually driven dynamical model of bimanual rhythmic movement (and phase perception). *Ecological Psychology, 16*(1), 45–53.

Blau, J. J. C., & Wagman, J. B. (2023). *Introduction to ecological psychology: A lawful approach to perceiving, acting, and cognizing.* New York: Routledge.

Brancazio, N., & Segundo-Ortin, M. (2020). Distal engagement: Intentions in perception. *Consciousness and Cognition, 79,* 102897. https://doi.org/10.1016/j.concog.2020.102897.

Bruineberg, J., Chemero, A., & Rietveld, E. (2018). General ecological information supports engagement with affordances for "higher" cognition. *Synthese, 196,* 5231–5251.

Bruineberg, J., & Rietveld, E. (2019). What's inside your head once you've figured out what your head's inside of. *Ecological Psychology, 31*(3), 198–217.

Cancar, L., Díaz, A., Barrientos, A., Travieso, D., & Jacobs, D. M. (2013). Tactile-sight: A sensory substitution device based on distance-related vibrotactile flow. *International Journal of Advanced Robotic Systems, 10*(6), 272. https://doi.org/10.5772/56235.

Carello, C., & Turvey, M. T. (2019). Challenging the axioms of perception: The retinal image and the visibility of light. In J. Wagman & J. Blau (Eds.), *Perception as Information Detection* (pp. 51–69). New York: Routledge.

Chemero, A. (2003). An outline of a theory of affordances. *Ecological Psychology, 15*(2), 181–195.

Chemero, A. (2009). *Radical embodied cognitive science.* Cambridge, MA: MIT.

Cisek, P. (2007). Cortical mechanisms of action selection: The affordance competition hypothesis. *Philosophical Transactions of the Royal Society B, 362*(1485), 1585–1599.

Clark, A. (2016). *Surfing uncertainty: Prediction, action, and the embodied mind.* Oxford: Oxford University Press.

Costall, A. (1995). Socializing affordances. *Theory & Psychology, 5*(4), 467–481. https://doi.org/10.1177/0959354395054001.

Costall, A. (2012). Canonical affordances in context. *Avant: Trends in Interdisciplinary Studies, 3*(2), 85–93.

Costall, A., & Morris, P. (2015). The "textbook Gibson": The assimilation of dissidence. *History of Psychology, 18*(1), 1–14.

Craig, C. M., Delay, D., Grealy, M. A., & Lee, D. N. (2000). Guiding the swing in golf putting. *Nature, 405,* 295–296.

Craig, C. M., & Lee, D. N. (1999). Neonatal control of nutritive sucking pressure: Evidence for an intrinsic τ-guide. *Experimental Brain Research, 124,* 371–382.

Craig, C., Pepping, G. J., & Grealy, M. (2005). Intercepting beats in predesignated target zones. *Experimental Brain Research, 165,* 490–504.

Crowther, R., Pohlmann, J., & Davids, K. (2016). An ecological dynamics framework for rehabilitation of multifidus atrophy and fatty infiltration: A case study. *Research to Practice, 2016.* Exercise & Sports Science Australia (ESSA), Melbourne.

Cutting, J. E. (1978). Generation of synthetic male and female walkers through manipulation of a biomechanical invariant. *Perception, 7*(4), 393–405. https://doi.org/10.1068/p070393.

Cutting, J. E. (1982). Two ecological perspectives: Gibson vs. Shaw and Turvey. *American Journal of Psychology, 95*(2), 199–222.

Davids, K., Araújo, D., Seifert, L., & Orth, D. (2015). Expert performance in sport: An ecological dynamics perspective. In J. Baker & D. Farrow (Eds.), *Routledge handbook of sport expertise* (pp. 130–144). New York: Routledge.

Davids, K., Araújo, D., Vilar, L., Renshaw, I., & Pinder, R. (2013). An ecological dynamics approach to skill acquisition: Implications for development of talent in sport. *Talent Development and Excellence, 5*(1), 21–34.

Davids, K., Button, C., & Bennett, S. (2008). *Dynamics of skill acquisition: A constraints-led approach.* Champaign, IL: Human Kinetics.

Davis, T. J., Riley, M. A., Shockley, K., & Cummins-Sebree, S. (2010). Perceiving affordances for joint actions. *Perception, 39*(12), *1624–1644.* https://doi.org/10.1068/p6712.

Dewey, J. (1896). The reflex arc concept in psychology. *Psychological Review, 3,* 357–370.

Dewey, J. (1922[2007]). *Human nature and conduct: An introduction to social psychology.* New York: Cosimo.

van Dijk, L., & Kiverstein, J. (2020). Direct perception in context: Radical empiricist reflections on the medium. *Synthese*. https://doi.org/10.1007/s11229-020-02578-3.

van Dijk, L., Withagen, R., & Bongers, R. M. (2015). Information without content: A Gibsonian reply to enactivists' worries. *Cognition, 134*, 210–214.

Djebbara, Z. (2022). *Affordances in everyday life*. London: Springer International.

Dotov, D. G. (2014). Putting reins on the brain: How the body and environment use it. *Frontiers in Human Neuroscience*, 8, 795. https://doi.org/10.3389/fnhum.2014.00795.

Duarte, R., Araújo, D., Correia, V., Davids, K., Marques, P., & Richardson, M. J. (2013). Competing together: Assessing the dynamics of team–team and player–team synchrony in professional association football. *Human Movement Science, 32*(4), 555–566. https://doi.org/10.1016/j.humov.2013.01.011.

Fajen, B. R. (2008). Perceptual learning and the visual control of braking. *Perception & Psychophysics, 70*(6), 1117–1129. https://doi.org/10.3758/PP.70.6.1117.

Fajen, B. R. (2021). *Visual control of locomotion*. Cambridge, UK: Cambridge University Press. https://doi.org/10.1017/9781108870474.

Fajen, B. R., & Warren, W. H. (2003). Behavioral dynamics of steering, obstacle avoidance, and route selection. *Journal of Experimental Psychology: Human Perception and Performance, 29*, 343–362.

Falandays, J. B., Yoshimi, J., Warren, W. H., & Spivey, M. J. (2023). A potential mechanism for Gibsonian resonance: Behavioral entrainment emerges from local homeostasis in an unsupervised reservoir network. *Cognitive Neurodynamics*, https://doi.org/10.1007/s11571-023-09988-2.

Favela, L. H. (2021). The dynamical renaissance in neuroscience. *Synthese, 199*, 2103–2127.

Fernandez, L., & Bootsma, R. J. (2008). Non-linear gaining in precision aiming: Making Fitts' task a bit easier. *Acta Psychologica, 129*(2), 217–227. https://doi.org/10.1016/j.actpsy.2008.06.001.

Field, D. T., & Wann, J. P. (2005). Perceiving time to collision activates the sensorimotor cortex. *Current Biology, 15*, 453–458.

Franchak, J. M., & Adolph, K. E. (2014). Gut estimates: Pregnant women adapt to changing possibilities for squeezing through doorways. *Attention, Perception, & Psychophysics, 76*, 460–472. https://doi.org/10.3758/s13414-013-0578-y.

Franchak, J. M., Celano, E. C., & Adolph, K. E. (2012). Perception of passage through openings depends on the size of the body in motion. *Experimental Brain Research, 223*(2), 301–310. https://doi.org/10.1007/s00221-012-3261-y.

Fultot, M., Frazier, P. A., Turvey, M. T., & Carello, C. (2019). What are nervous systems for? *Ecological Psychology, 31*(3), 218–234.

Georgopoulos, A. P. (2007). A tribute to tau. In G. Pepping, & M. A., Grealy (Eds.), *Closing the gap: The scientific writings of David N. Lee* (pp. 157–161). Mahwah, NJ: Lawrence Erlbaum.

Giblin, G., Farrow, D., Reid, M., Ball, K., & Abernethy, B. (2015). Exploring the kinaesthetic sensitivity of skilled performers for implementing movement instructions. *Human Movement Science, 41*, 76–91.

Gibson, E. J. (1963). Perceptual learning. *Annual Review of Psychology, 14*(1), 29–56. https://doi.org/10.1146/annurev.ps.14.020163.000333.

Gibson, E. J. (1969). *Principles of perceptual learning and development*. Hoboken, NJ: Prentice-Hall.

Gibson, E. J. (1991). *An odyssey in learning and perception*. Cambridge, MA: MIT.

Gibson, E. J. (1994). Has psychology a future? *Psychological Science, 5*(2), 69–76. https://doi.org/10.1111/j.1467-9280.1994.tb00633.x.

Gibson, E. J. (1997). An ecological psychologist's prolegomena for perceptual development: A functional approach. In C. Dent-Read & P. Zukow-Goldring (Eds.), *Evolving explanations of development: Ecological approaches to organism–environment systems.* (pp. 23–45). *American Psychological Association.* https://doi.org/10.1037/10265-001.

Gibson, E. J. (2000). Perceptual learning in development: Some basic concepts. *Ecological Psychology, 12*(4), 295–302. https://doi.org/10.1207/S15326969ECO1204_04.

Gibson, E. J. (2001). *Perceiving the affordances: A portrait of two psychologists*. Mahwah, NJ: Lawrence Erlbaum.

Gibson, E. J., & Pick, A. D. (2000). *An ecological approach to perceptual learning and development*. Oxford, UK: Oxford University Press.

Gibson, E. J., & Rader, N. (1979). Attention. In G. A. Hale & M. Lewis (Eds.), *Attention and cognitive development* (pp. 1–21). New York: Springer. https://doi.org/10.1007/978-1-4613-2985-5_1.

Gibson, E. J., & Walk, R. D. (1960). The "Visual Cliff." *Scientific American, 202*(4), 64–71.

Gibson, E. J., & Walker, A. S. (1984). Development of knowledge of visual-tactual affordances of substance. *Child Development, 55*(2), 453–460.

Gibson, J. J. (1933). Adaptation, after-effect and contrast in the perception of curved lines. *Journal of Experimental Psychology, 16*, 1–31.

Gibson, J. J. (1950a). *The perception of the visual world*. Cambridge, MA: Riverside.

Gibson, J. J. (1950b). The implications of learning theory for social psychology. In J. G. Miller (Ed.), *Experiments in social process: A symposium on social psychology* (pp. 149–167). New York: McGraw-Hill.

Gibson, J. J. (1960). The concept of the stimulus in psychology. *American Psychologist, 15*, 694–703. https://doi.org/10.1037/h0047037.

Gibson, J. J. (1966). *The senses considered as perceptual systems.* Boston: Houghton Mifflin.

Gibson, J. J. (1967[1982]). Autobiography. In E. S. Reed & R. Jones (Eds.), *Reasons for realism* (pp. 7–22). Hillsdale, NJ: Lawrence Erlbaum.

Gibson, J. J. (1970a[1982]). On theories for visual space perception. In E. S. Reed & R. Jones (Eds.), *Reasons for realism* (pp. 76–89). Hillsdale, NJ: Lawrence Erlbaum.

Gibson, J. J. (1970b[1982]). A history of the ideas behind ecological optics: Introductory remarks on ecological optics. In E. S. Reed & R. Jones (Eds.), *Reasons for realism* (pp. 90–101). Hillsdale, NJ: Lawrence Erlbaum.

Gibson, J. J. (1972[1982]). Unpublished material. In E. S. Reed & R. Jones (Eds.), *Reasons for realism* (pp. 348–349), Hillsdale, NJ: Lawrence Erlbaum.

Gibson, J. J. (1979[1982]). What is involved in surface perception? In E. S. Reed & R. Jones (Eds.), *Reasons for realism* (pp. 106–112), Hillsdale, NJ: Lawrence Erlbaum.

Gibson, J. J. (1979[2015]). *The ecological approach to visual perception.* New York: Psychology Press.

Gibson, J. J., & Crooks, L. E. (1938). A theoretical field-analysis of automobile-driving. *American Journal of Psychology, 51*(3), 453. https://doi.org/10.2307/1416145.

Gibson, J. J., & Gibson, E. J. (1955). Perceptual learning: Differentiation or enrichment? *Psychological Review, 62*, 32–42.

Gibson, J. J., & Waddell, D. (1952). Homogeneous retinal stimulation and visual perception. *American Journal of Psychology, 65*(2), 263–270. https://doi.org/10.2307/1418360.

Gray, R. (2021). *How we learn to move: A revolution in the way we coach and practice sports skills.* Perception and Action Consulting & Education, LLC.

Haken, H., Kelso, J. A. S., & Bunz, H. (1985). A theoretical model of phase transitions in human hand movements. *Biological Cybernetics, 51*, 347–356.

Hasson, U., Nastase, S. A., & Goldstein, A. (2020). Direct fit to nature: An evolutionary perspective on biological and artificial neural networks. *Neuron, 105*(3), 416–434.

Heft, H. (1989). Affordances and the body: An intentional analysis of Gibson's ecological approach to visual perception. *Journal for the Theory of Social Behaviour, 19*(1), 1–30. https://doi.org/10.1111/j.1468-5914.1989 .tb00133.x.

Heft, H. (2001). *Ecological psychology in context: James Gibson, Roger Barker, and the legacy of William James's radical empiricism.* Mahwah, NJ: Lawrence Erlbaum.

Heft, H. (2003). Affordances, dynamic experience, and the challenge of reification. *Ecological Psychology, 15*(2), 149–180. https://doi.org/10.1207/ S15326969ECO1502_4.

Heft, H. (2017). Perceptual information of "an entirely different order": The "cultural environment" in *The Senses Considered as Perceptual Systems. Ecological Psychology, 29*(2), 122–145. https://doi.org/10.1080/10407413 .2017.1297187.

Heft, H. (2018). Places: Widening the scope of an ecological approach to perception–action with an emphasis on child development. *Ecological Psychology, 30*(1), 99–123.

Heft, H. (2019). Revisiting "The discovery of the occluding edge and its implications for perception" 40 years on. In J. B. Wagman & J. J. C. Blau (Eds.), *Perception as information detection: Reflections on Gibson's ecological approach to visual perception* (pp. 151–173). New York: Routledge.

Heft, H. (2020). Ecological psychology as social psychology? *Theory & Psychology, 30*(6), 813–826. https://doi.org/10.1177/0959354320934545.

Heft, H., Hoch, J., Edmunds, T., & Weeks, J. (2014). Can the identity of a behavior setting be perceived through patterns of joint action? An investigation of place perception. *Behavioral Sciences, 4*(4), 371–393. https://doi .org/10.3390/bs4040371.

Heras-Escribano, M. (2019). *The philosophy of affordances.* Cham: Palgrave Macmillan.

Hill, S. C. (2017). Toward conceptualizing race and racial identity development within an attractor landscape. *SAGE Open, 7*(3), https://doi.org/10.1177/ 2158244017719310.

Hodges, B. H., & Baron, R. M. (2007). On making social psychology more ecological and ecological psychology more social. *Ecological Psychology, 19*(2), 79–84. https://doi.org/10.1080/10407410701331918.

Hodges, B. H., & Rączaszek-Leonardi, J. (2022). Ecological values theory: Beyond conformity, goal-seeking, and rule-following in action and interaction. *Review of General Psychology, 26*(1), 86–103. https://doi.org/ 10.1177/10892680211048174.

Hohwy, J. (2013). *The predictive mind.* Oxford: Oxford University Press.

Holden J. G., Riley M., Gao J., & Torre K. (2013). Fractal analyses: Statistical and methodological innovations and best practices. *Frontiers in Physiology.* http://doi.org/10.3389/fphys.2013.00097.

Holt, E. B. (1915a). Response and cognition I: The specific response relation. *Journal of Philosophy, Psychology and Scientific Methods, 12,* 365–373.

Holt, E. B. (1915b). *The Freudian wish and its place in ethics.* New York: H. Holt.

Hull, C. L. (1943). *Principles of behavior: An introduction to behavior theory.* New York: Appleton.

Jacobs, D. M., & Michaels, C. F. (2007). Direct learning. *Ecological Psychology, 19*(4), 321–349.

James, W. (1890). *The principles of psychology (Vols. 1 & 2).* New York: Dover.

Johansson, G. (1973). Visual perception of biological motion and a model for its analysis. *Perception & Psychophysics, 14*(2), 201–211. https://doi.org/10.3758/BF03212378.

Kayed, N. S., Farstad, H., & Van der Meer, A. L. H. (2008). Preterm infants' timing strategies to optical collisions. *Early Human Development, 84,* 381–388.

Käufer, S., & Chemero, A. (2015). *Phenomenology: An introduction.* Malden, MA: Polity.

Kelso, J. A. S. (1995). *Dynamic patterns.* Cambridge, MA: MIT.

Kiefer, A. W., Kushner, A. M., Groene, J., Williams, C., Riley, M. A., & Myer, G. D. (2015). A commentary on real-time biofeedback to augment neuromuscular training for ACL injury prevention in adolescent athletes. *Journal of Sports Science & Medicine, 14*(1), 1.

Kinsella-Shaw, J. M., Shaw, B., & Turvey, M. T. (1992). Perceiving "walk-on-able" Slopes. *Ecological Psychology, 4*(4), *223–239.* https://doi.org/10.1207/s15326969eco0404_2.

Koffka, K. (1935). *Principles of Gestalt psychology.* San Diego, CA: Harcourt, Brace.

Konczak, J., Meeuwsen, H. J., & Cress, M. E. (1992). Changing affordances in stair climbing: The perception of maximum climbability in young and older adults. *Journal of Experimental Psychology: Human Perception and Performance, 18*(3), 691–697. https://doi.org/10.1037/0096-1523.18.3.691.

Kono, T. (2009). Social affordances and the possibility of ecological linguistics. *Integrative Psychological and Behavioral Science, 43*(4), 356–373. https://doi.org/10.1007/s12124-009-9097-8.

Kretch, K. S., & Adolph, K. E. (2013). Cliff or step? Posture-specific learning at the edge of a drop-off. *Child development, 84*(1), 226–240. https://doi.org/10.1111/j.1467-8624.2012.01842.x.

Kugler, P. N., & Turvey, M. T. (1987). *Information, natural law, and the self-assembly of rhythmic movement*. Hillsdale: Lawrence Erlbaum.

van de Langenberg, R., Kingma, I., & Beek, P. J. (2007). Perception of limb orientation in the vertical plane depends on center of mass rather than inertial eigenvectors. *Experimental Brain Research*, 180, 595–607.

Lee, D. N. (2009). General tau theory: Evolution to date. *Perception, 38,* 837–858.

Lee, D. N., Lishman, J. R., & Thomson, J. A. (1982). Regulation of gait in long jumping. *Journal of Experimental Psychology: Human Perception and Performance, 8*(3), 448–459.

Lee, D., Port, N. L., Kruse, W., & Georgopoulos, A. P. (2001). Neuronal clusters in the primate motor cortex during interceptin of moving targets. *Journal of Cognitive Neuroscience, 13*, 319–331.

Lee, D. N., & Reddish, P. E. (1981). Plummeting gannets: A paradigm of ecological optics. *Nature 293*, 293–294.

Lee, Y., Lee, S., Carello, C., & Turvey, M. T. (2012). An archer's perceived form scales the "hitableness" of archery targets. *Journal of Experimental Psychology: Human Perception and Performance, 38*(5), 1125–1131. https://doi.org/10.1037/a0029036.

Lewin, L. (1931). The conflict between Aristotelian and Galileian modes of thought in contemporary psychology. *Journal of General Psychology, 5*(2), 141–177.

Lobo, L., Nordbeck, P. C., Raja, V., et al. (2019). Route selection and obstacle avoidance with a short-range haptic sensory substitution device. *International Journal of Human-Computer Studies*. https://doi.org/10.1016/j.ijhcs.2019.03.004.

Lobo, L., Travieso, D., Barrientos, A., & Jacobs, D. M. (2014). Stepping on obstacles with a sensory substitution device on the lower leg: Practice without vision is more beneficial than practice with vision. *PLOS ONE, 9* (6), e98801. https://doi.org/10.1371/journal.pone.0098801.

Mace, W. (1977). James J. Gibson's strategy for perceiving: Ask not what's inside your head, but what's your head inside of. In R. Shaw & J. Bransford (Eds.), *Perceiving, acting, and knowing: Toward an ecological psychology* (pp. 43–65). Hillsdale, NJ: Lawrence Erlbaum.

Madruga-Parera, M., Bishop, C., Fort-Vanmeerhaeghe, A., Beato, M., Gonzalo-Skok, O., Romero-Rodríguez, D. (2022). Effects of 8 weeks of isoinertial vs. cable-resistance training on motor skills performance and interlimb asymmetries. *Journal of Strength and Conditioning Research*, 36(5), 1200–1208.

Marr, D. (1982). *Vision: A computational investigation into the human representation and processing of visual information.* Cambridge, MA: MIT.

Marsh, K. L., Johnston, L., Richardson, M. J., & Schmidt, R. C. (2009). Toward a radically embodied, embedded social psychology. *European Journal of Social Psychology, 39*(7), 1217–1225. https://doi.org/10.1002/ejsp.666.

Marsh, K. L., Richardson, M. J., Baron, R. M., & Schmidt, R. C. (2006). Contrasting approaches to perceiving and acting with others. *Ecological Psychology, 18*(1), 1–38. https://doi.org/10.1207/s15326969eco1801_1.

Matthis, J. S., Muller, K. S., Bonnen, K. L., & Hayhoe, M. M. (2022) Retinal optic flow during natural locomotion. *PLoS ONE Computational Biology, 18* (2), e1009575. https://doi.org/10.1371/journal.pcbi.1009575.

McArthur, L. Z., & Baron, R. M. (1983). Toward an ecological theory of social perception. *Psychological Review, 90*(3), 215–238. https://doi.org/10.1037/0033-295X.90.3.215.

van der Meer, A. L. H., Svantesson, M., & van der Weel, F. R. (2012). Longitudinal study of looming in infants with high-density EEG. *Developmental Neuroscience, 34*(6), 488–501. https://doi.org/10.1159/000345154.

van der Meer, A. L. H., & van der Weel, F. R. (2019). The optical information for self-perception in development. In J. Wagman & J. Blau (Eds.), *Perception as information detection* (pp. 110–129). New York: Routledge.

van der Meer, A. L. H., van der Weel, F. R., & Lee, D. N. (1994). Prospective control in catching by infants. *Perception, 23*(3), 287–302. https://doi.org/10.1068/p230287.

Merchant, H., Battaglia-Mayer, A., & Georgopoulos, A. P. (2003a). Interception of real and apparent motion targets: Psychophysics in humans and monkeys. *Experimental Brain Research, 152,* 106–112.

Merchant, H., Battaglia-Mayer, A., & Georgopoulos, A. P. (2003b). Functional organization of parietal neuronal responses to optic-flow stimuli. *Journal of Neurophysiology, 90,* 675–682.

Merchant, H., Battaglia-Mayer, A., & Georgopoulos, A. P. (2004). Neural responses during interception of real and apparent circularly moving stimuli in motor cortex and area 7a. *Cerebral Cortex, 14,* 314–331.

Merchant, H., & Georgopoulos, A. P. (2006). Neurophysiology of perceptual and motor aspects of interception. *Journal of Neurophysiology, 95,* 1–13.

Michaels, C. F., & Carello, C. (1981). *Direct perception.* Englewood Cliffs, NJ: Prentice-Hall.

Michotte, A. (1946). *La perception de la causalité.* Louvain: Études de Psychologie.

Nalepka, P., Kallen, R. W., Chemero, A., Saltzman, E., & Richardson, M. J. (2017). Herd those sheep: Emergent multiagent coordination and behavioral-mode switching. *Psychological Science, 28*(5), 630–650.

Nalepka, P., Lamb, M., Kallen, R. W., Shockley, K., Chemero, A., Saltzman, E., et al. (2019). Human social motor solutions for human–machine interaction in dynamical task contexts. *Proceedings of the National Academy of Science (PNAS), 116*(4), 1437–1446.

Neisser, U. (1967). *Cognitive psychology*. New York: Appleton-Century-Crofts.

Neisser, U. (1976). *Cognition and reality: Principles and implications of cognitive psychology*. New York: W. H. Freeman/Times Books/Henry Holt.

Newell, K., Liu, Y.-T., & Mayer-Kress, G. (2008). Landscapes beyond the HKB model. In A. Fuchs & V. K. Jirsa (Eds.), *Coordination: Neural, behavioral and social dynamics* (pp. 27–44). Berlin: Springer.

Newen, A., De Bruin, L., & Gallagher, S. (2018). *The Oxford handbook of 4E cognition*. Oxford: Oxford University Press.

van Orden, G. C., Holden, J. G., & Turvey, M. T. (2003). Self-organization of cognitive performance. *Journal of Experimental Psychology: General, 132* (3), 331–350.

van Orden, G. C., Hollis, G., & Wallot, S. (2012). The blue-collar brain. *Frontiers in Psychology, 3*, art. 207.

Pagano, C. C., & Turvey, M. T. (1995). The inertia tensor as a basis for the perception of limb orientation. *Journal of experimental psychology. Human perception and performance, 21*(5), 1070–1087.

Pedersen, S., & Bang, J. (2016). Historicizing affordance theory: A rendezvous between ecological psychology and cultural-historical activity theory. *Theory & Psychology, 26*(6), 731–750. https://doi.org/10.1177/0959354316669021.

Pezzulo, G., & Cisek, P. (2016). Navigating the affordance landscape: Feedback control as a process model of behavior and cognition. *Trends in Cognitive Sciences, 20*(6), 414–424.

Pijpers, J. R., Oudejans, R. R. D., & Bakker, F. C. (2007). Changes in the perception of action possibilities while climbing to fatigue on a climbing wall. *Journal of Sports Sciences, 25*(1), 97–110. https://doi.org/10.1080/02640410600630894.

Pillai, A. S., & Jirsa, V. K. (2017). Symmetry breaking in space–time hierarchies shapes brain dynamics and behavior. *Neuron, 94*, 1010–1026.

Pinder, R. A., Davids, K., Renshaw, I., & Araújo, D. (2011). Representative learning design and functionality of research and practice in sport. *Journal of Sport and Exercise Psychology, 33*(1), 146–155. https://doi.org/10.1123/jsep.33.1.146.

Port, N. L., Kruse, W., Lee, D., & Georgopoulos, A. P. (2001). Motor cortical activity duringinterception of moving targets. *Journal of Cognitive Neuroscience, 13*, 306–318. https://doi.org/10.1162/08989290151137368.

Port, R. (2003). Meter and speech. *Journal of Phonetics, 31*, 599–611.

Rader, N. de V. (2018). Uniting Jimmy and Jackie: Foundation for a research program in developmental ecological psychology. *Ecological Psychology, 30* (2), 129–145. https://doi.org/10.1080/10407413.2018.1439110.

Ramstead M. J. D., Sakthivadivel D. A. R., Heins C., et al. (2023). On Bayesian mechanics: A physics of and by beliefs. *Interface Focus*, http://doi.org/10.1098/rsfs.2022.0029.

Raja, V. (2018). A theory of resonance: Toward an ecological cognitive architecture. *Minds and Machines, 28*(1), 29–51.

Raja, V. (2019a). J. J. Gibson's most radical idea: The development of a new law-based psychology. *Theory & Psychology, 29*(6), 789–806.

Raja, V. (2019b). From metaphor to theory: The role of resonance in perceptual learning. *Adaptive Behavior, 27*(6), 405–421.

Raja, V. (2021). Resonance and radical embodiment. *Synthese*, https://doi.org/10.1007/s11229-020-02610-6.

Raja, V., & Anderson, M. L. (2019). Radical embodied cognitive neuroscience. *Ecological Psychology, 31*(2), 166–181.

Raja, V., & Anderson, M. L. (2021). Behavior considered as an enabling constraint. In F. Calzavarini and M. Viola (Eds.), *Neural mechanisms: New challenges in the philosophy of neuroscience* (pp. 209–232). New York: Springer.

Raja, V., Biener, Z., & Chemero, A. (2017). From Kepler to Gibson. *Ecological Psychology*, 29(2), 1–15.

Raja, V., Valluri, D., Baggs, E., Chemero, A., & Anderson, M. L. (2021). The Markov blanket trick: On the scope of the free energy principle and active inference. *Physics of Life Reviews, 39*, 49–72.

Reed, E. S. (1988). *James J. Gibson and the psychology of perception*. New Haven, CT: Yale University Press.

Reed, E. S. (1993). The intention to use a specific affordance: A conceptual framework for psychology. In: R. H. Wozniak and K. W. Fischer (Eds.), *Development in context: Acting and thinking in specific environments* (pp. 45–76), New York: Psychology Press.

Reed, E. S. (1996). *Encountering the world: Toward an ecological psychology*. Oxford: Oxford University Press.

Reed, E. S., & Jones, R. (1982). *Reasons for realism: Selected essays of James J. Gibson*. Hillsdale, NJ: Lawrence Erlbaum.

Regia-Corte, T., & Wagman, J. B. (2008). Perception of affordances for standing on an inclined surface depends on height of center of mass. *Experimental Brain Research, 191*(1), 25–35. https://doi.org/10.1007/s00221-008-1492-8.

Richardson, M. J., Marsh, K. L., & Baron, R. M. (2007). Judging and actualizing intrapersonal and interpersonal affordances. *Journal of Experimental Psychology: Human Perceptions & Performance, 33*, 845–859.

Richardson, M. J., Marsh, K. L., Isenhower, R. W., Goodman, J. R. L., & Schmidt, R. C. (2007). Rocking together: Dynamics of intentional and unintentional interpersonal coordination. *Human Movement Science, 26*(6), 867–891. https://doi.org/10.1016/j.humov.2007.07.002.

Rietveld, E., & Kiverstein, J. (2014). A rich landscape of affordances. *Ecological Psychology, 26*(4), 325–352. https://doi.org/10.1080/10407413.2014 .958035.

Riley, M., & van Orden, G. C. (2005). *Tutorials in contemporary nonlinear methods for the behavioral sciences.* http://www.nsf.gov/sbe/bcs/pac/nmbs/nmbs.jsp.

Riley, M., Richardson, M., Shockley, K., & Ramenzoni, V. (2011). Interpersonal synergies. *Frontiers in Psychology, 2.* https://www.frontier sin.org/articles/10.3389/fpsyg.2011.00038.

Rio, K. W., Dachner, G. C., & Warren, W. H. (2018). Local interactions underlying collective motion in human crowds. *Proceedings of the Royal Society B, Biological Sciences.* https://doi.org/10.1098/rspb.2018.0611.

de Rugy, A., Taga, G., Montagne, G., Buekers, M. J., & Laurent, M. (2002). Perception–action coupling model for human locomotor pointing. *Biological Cybernetics, 87*, 141–150.

Ryan, K. J., & Gallagher, S. (2020). Between ecological psychology and enactivism: Is there resonance? *Frontiers in Psychology.* https://doi.org/ 10.3389/fpsyg.2020.01147.

Savelsbergh, G. J. P., Williams, A. M., Kamp, J. V. D., & Ward, P. (2002). Visual search, anticipation and expertise in soccer goalkeepers. *Journal of Sports Sciences, 20*(3), 279–287. https://doi.org/10.1080/026404102317284826.

Schmidt, R., & Richardson, M. (2008). Dynamics of interpersonal coordination. In A. Fuchs & V. K. Jirsa (Eds.), *Coordination: Neural, behavioral, and social dynamics* (pp. 282–308). Berlin: Springer.

Schneider, K., Zernicke, R. F., Schmidt, R. A., & Hart, T. J. (1989). Changes in limb dynamics during the practice of rapid arm movements. *Journal of Biomechanics, 22*(8–9), 805–817.

Schögler, B., Pepping, G. J., & Lee, D. N. (2008). TauG-guidance of transients in expressive musical performance. *Experimental Brain Research, 198*: 361–372.

Sedgwick, H. A. (1973). The visible horizon: A potential source of visual information for the perception of size and distance. Doctoral Dissertation, Cornell University. Dissertation Abstracts International, 34, 1301B–1302B (University Microfilms No. 73-22530).

Sedgwick, H. A. (2001). J. J. Gibson's "ground theory of space perception." *i-Perception*, *12*(3), 1–55.

Segundo-Ortin, M. (2019). *Toward a radical enactive cognitive science*. University of Wollongong Thesis Collection 2017. https://ro.uow.edu.au/theses1/691.

Segundo-Ortin, M. (2020). Agency from a radical embodied standpoint: An ecological-enactive proposal. *Frontiers in Psychology*, *11*. https://doi.org/10.3389/fpsyg.2020.01319.

Segundo-Ortin, M. (2022). Socio-cultural norms in ecological psychology: The education of intention. *Phenomenology and the Cognitive Sciences*. https://doi.org/10.1007/s11097-022-09807-9.

Segundo-Ortin, M., & Heras-Escribano, M. (2021). Neither mindful nor mindless, but minded: Habits, ecological psychology, and skilled performance. *Synthese*. https://doi.org/10.1007/s11229-021-03238-w.

Segundo-Ortin, M., & Heras-Escribano, M. (2023). The risk of trivializing affordances: Mental and cognitive affordances examined. *Philosophical Psychology*. https://doi.org/10.1080/09515089.2023.2228341.

Segundo-Ortin, M., Heras-Escribano, M., & Raja, V. (2019). Ecological psychology is radical enough: A reply to radical enactivists. *Philosophical Psychology*, *32*(7), 1001–1023. https://doi.org/10.1080/09515089.2019.1668238.

Segundo-Ortin, M., & Kalis, A. (2022). Intentions in ecological psychology: An Anscombean proposal. *Review of Philosophy and Psychology*. https://doi.org/10.1007/s13164-022-00661-x.

Segundo-Ortin, M., & Satne, G. (2022). Sharing attention, sharing affordances: From dyadic interaction to collective information. In M. Wehrle, D. D'Angelo, & E. Solomonova (Eds.), *Access and Mediation* (pp. 91–112). De Gruyter. https://doi.org/10.1515/9783110647242-005.

Shockley, K., Carello, C., & Turvey, M. T. (2004). Metamers in the haptic perception of heaviness and moveableness. *Perception & Psychophysics*, *66* (5), 731–742. https://doi.org/10.3758/BF03194968.

Silva, P., Keifer, A., Riley, M. A., & Chemero, A. (2019). Trading perception and action for complex cognition: Application of theoretical principles from ecological psychology to the design of interventions for skill learning. In M. Cappuccio (Ed.), *Handbook of embodied cognition and sport psychology* (pp. 47–74), Cambridge, MA: MIT.

Snow, J. C., & Culham, J. C. (2022). The treachery of images: How realism influences brain and behavior. *Trends in Cognitive Science*, *25*(6), 506–519.

Solomon, H. Y., & Turvey, M. T. (1988). Haptically perceiving the distances reachable with hand-held objects. *Journal of experimental psychology. Human perception and performance*, *14 3*, 404–427.

Stadler, M., & Kruse, P. (1990). The self-organization perspective in cognition research: Historical remarks and new experimental approaches. In H. Haken and M. Stadler (Eds.), *Synergetics of Cognition* (pp. 32–52). Berlin: Springer Verlag.

Stoffregen, T. A. (2003). Affordances as properties of the animal-environment system. *Ecological Psychology*, *15*(2), 115–134.

Stoffregen, T., Yang, C.-M., Giveans, M., Flanagan, M., & Bardy, B. (2009). Movement in the perception of an affordance for wheelchair locomotion. *Ecological Psychology*, *21*, 1–36. https://doi.org/10.1080/10407410802 626001.

Strogatz, S. H. (1994). *Nonlinear dynamics and chaos*. Reading, MA: Perseus.

Sun, H., & Frost, B. J. (1998). Computation of different optical variables of looming objects in pigeon nucleus rotundus neurons. *Nature Neuroscience*, *1*, 296–303.

Swanson, L. W. (2015). *Neuroanatomical terminology: A lexicon of classical origins and historical foundations*. Oxford: Oxford University Press.

Szokolszky, A. (2003). An interview with Eleanor Gibson. *Ecological Psychology*, *15*(4), 271–281. https://doi.org/10.1207/s15326969eco1504_2.

Tan, H.-R. M., Leuthold, A. C., Lee, D. N., Lynch, J. K., & Georgopoulos, A. P. (2009). Neural mechanisms of movement speed and tau as revealed by magnetoencephalography. *Experimental Brain Research*, *195*, 541–552.

Thomas, B. J., Jeffrey B., Riley, M. A., & Wagman, J. B. (2019). Information and its detection: The consequences of Gibson's Theory of information pickup. In J. Wagman & J. Blau (Eds.), *Perception as information detection* (pp. 237–251). New York: Routledge.

Titchener, E. B. (1898). The postulates of a structural psychology. *Philosophical Review*, *7*(5), 449–465.

Tognoli, E., & Kelso, J. A. S. (2014). The metastable brain. *Neuron*, *81*, 35–48.

Tognoli E., Zhang M., Fuchs A., Beetle C., & Kelso J. A. S. (2020). Coordination dynamics: A foundation for understanding social behavior. *Frontiers in Human Neuroscience*. http://doi.org/10.3389/fnhum.2020 .00317.

Travassos, B., Araújo, D., Davids, K., Vilar, L., Esteves, P., & Vanda, C. (2012). Informational constraints shape emergent functional behaviours during performance of interceptive actions in team sports. *Psychology of Sport and Exercise, 13*(2), 216–223. https://doi.org/10.1016/j.psychsport .2011.11.009.

Tsao, T., & Tsao, D. Y. (2022). A topological solution to object segmentation and tracking. *Proceedings of the National Academy of Science (PNAS)*, 119, e2204248119. https://doi.org/10.1073/pnas.2204248119.

Turvey, M. T. (1992). Affordances and prospective control: An outline of the ontology. *Ecological Psychology, 4*(3), 173–187.

Turvey, M. T. (2019). *Lectures on perception: An ecological approach.* New York: Routledge.

Turvey, M. T., & Fonseca, S. (2014). The medium of haptic perception: A tensegrity hypothesis. *Journal of Motor Behavior, 46*(3), 143–187.

Turvey, M. T., Shaw, R., Reed, E. S., & Mace, W. (1981). Ecological laws for perceiving and acting: A reply to Fodor and Pylyshyn. *Cognition, 10*, 237–304.

van der Weel, F. R., Sokolovskis, I., Raja, V., & van der Meer, A. L. H. (2022). Neural aspects of prospective control through resonating taus in an interceptive timing task. *Brain Sciences, 12*(12), 1737. https://doi.org/10.3390/ brainsci12121737.

Varoqui, D., Froger, J., Pélissier, J.-Y., & Bardy, B. G. (2011). Effect of coordination biofeedback on (re)learning preferred postural patterns in post-stroke patients. *Motor Control, 15*(2), 187–205. https://doi.org/ 10.1123/mcj.15.2.187.

Vaughan, J., Mallett, C. J., Potrac, P., López-Felip, M. A., & Davids, K. (2021). Football, culture, skill development and sport coaching: Extending ecological approaches in athlete development using the skilled intentionality framework. *Frontiers in Psychology, 12*, 635420. https://doi.org/10.3389/ fpsyg.2021.635420.

Vauclin, P., Wheat, J., Wagman, J. B., & Seifert, L. (2023). A systematic review of perception of affordances for the person-plus-object system. *Psychonomic Bulletin & Review.* https://doi.org/10.3758/s13423-023-02319-w.

Venkatraman, V., Lee, J., & Schwarz, C. (2016). Steer or brake? Modeling drivers' collision avoidance behavior using perceptual cues. *Transportation Research Record: Journal of the Transportation Research Board, 16–6657.* https://doi.org/10.3141/2602-12.

Vilhelmsen, K., Agyei, S. B., van der Weel, F. R. (Ruud), & van der Meer, A. L. H. (2019). A high-density EEG study of differentiation between two speeds and directions of simulated optic flow in adults and infants. *Psychophysiology, 56*(1), e13281. https://doi.org/10.1111/psyp.13281.

Wagemans, J., Elder, J. H., Kubovy, M., et al. (2012). A century of Gestalt psychology in visual perception: I. Perceptual grouping and figure-ground organization. Psychological Bulletin, *138*(6), 1172–1217.

Wagman, J. B. (2019). A guided tour of Gibson's theory of affordances. In J. Wagman & J. Blau (Eds.), *Perception as information detection* (pp. 130–148). New York: Routledge.

Wagman, J. B., Lozano, S., Jiménez, A. A., Covarrubias, P., & Cabrera, F. (2019). Perception of affordances in the animal kingdom and beyond. In I. Z. Riveros, F. Cabrera González, J. A. Camacho Candia, & E. C. Gutiérrez (Eds.), *Aproximaciones al estudio del comportamiento y sus aplicaciones (Volumen II)* (pp. 70–108), Ocotlán, Jalisco: Universidad de Guadalajara.

Wagman, J. B., Shockley, K., Riley, M. A., & Turvey, M. T. (2001). Attunement, calibration, and exploration in fast haptic perceptual learning. *Journal of Motor Behavior, 33*, 323–327.

Wagman, J. B., & Taylor, K. R. (2005). Perceiving affordances for aperture crossing for the person-plus-object system. *Ecological Psychology, 17*(2), 105–130. https://doi.org/10.1207/s15326969eco1702_3.

Walton, A. E., Richardson, M. J., Langland-Hassan, P., & Chemero, A. (2015). Improvisation and the self-organization of multiple musical bodies. *Frontiers in Psychology, 6*(6).

Wang, Y., & Frost, B. J. (1992). Time to collision is signalled by neurons in the nucleus rotundus of pigeons. *Nature, 356*, 236–238.

Warren, W. H. (1984). Perceiving affordances: Visual guidance of stair climbing. *Journal of Experimental Psychology: Human Perception and Performance, 10*(5), 683–703. https://doi.org/10.1037/0096-1523.10.5.683.

Warren, W. H. (1998). Visually controlled locomotion: 40 years later. *Ecological Psychology, 10*(3–4), 177–219.

Warren, W. H. (2006). The dynamics of perception and action. *Psychological Review*, 113(2), 358–389.

Warren, W. H. (2018). Collective motion in human crowds. *Current Directions in Psychological Science, 27*(4), 232–240. https://doi.org/10.1177/0963721 417746743.

Warren, W. H. (2019). Perceiving surface layout: Ground theory, affordances, and the objects of perception. In J. Wagman & J. Blau (Eds.), *Perception as information detection* (pp. 151–173). New York: Routledge.

Warren, W. H. (2021). Information is where you find it: Perception as an ecologically well-posed problem. *I-Perception*, 12(2). https://doi.org/10.1177/20416695211000366.

Warren, W. H., & Whang, S. (1987). Visual guidance of walking through apertures: Body-scaled information for affordances. *Journal of Experimental*

Psychology: Human Perception and Performance, 13, 371–383. https://doi .org/10.1037/0096-1523.13.3.371.

van der Weel, F. R., & van der Meer, A. L. H., (2009). Seeing it coming: Infants' brain responses to looming danger. *Naturwissenschaften*, *96*, 1385. https:// doi.org/10.1007/s00114-009-0585-y.

Wilson, A. D., Bingham, G. P. (2008). Identifying the information for the visual perception of relative phase. *Perception & Psychophysics*, 70, 465–476.

de Wit, M. M., de Vries, S., van der Kamp, J., & Withagen, R. (2017). Affordances and neuroscience: Steps toward a successful marriage. *Neuroscience & Biobehavioral Reviews*, *80*, 622–629.

Withagen, R., Araújo, D., & de Poel, H. J. (2017). Inviting affordances and agency. *New Ideas in Psychology*, 45, 11–18. https://doi.org/10.1016/j.newideapsych .2016.12.002.

Withagen, R., & Chemero, A. (2009). Naturalizing perception: Developing the Gibsonian approach to perception along evolutionary lines. *Theory & Psychology*, 19(3), 363–389.

Withagen, R., de Poel, H. J., Araújo, D., & Pepping, G.-J. (2012). Affordances can invite behavior: Reconsidering the relationship between affordances and agency. *New Ideas in Psychology*, 30(2), 250–258. https://doi.org/ 10.1016/j.newideapsych.2011.12.003.

Woods, C. T., McKeown, I., Rothwell, M., Araújo, D., Robertson, S., & Davids, K. (2020). Sport practitioners as sport ecology designers: How ecological dynamics has progressively changed perceptions of skill scquisi-tion in the sporting habitat. *Frontiers in Psychology*, 11. https://doi.org/ 10.3389/fpsyg.2020.00654.

Acknowledgments

We are thankful to the series editor Professor James Enns and other members of the editorial board for accepting our proposal to write this Elements and guiding us through the process, and also to three anonymous referees for their insightful comments and suggestions. We also thank Cecilio Hortelano for helping us design some of the figures, and Paco Calvo for his suggestions on improving the manuscript. Last but not least, we would like to thank our partners, Ana and Robyn, for being there and supporting us while we were fully engaged in this project. There is no space to state our gratitude.

Finally, we would like to dedicate this book to the memory of Professor Michael T. Turvey, who taught and trained so many generations of researchers interested in ecological psychology. The whole community is thankful for his immense contribution.

Miguel Segundo-Ortin was supported by a "Ramón y Cajal" Fellowship (Grant# RYC2021-031242-I) funded by MCIN/AEI/10.13039/501100011033 and by the European Union NextGenerationEU/PRTR. Vicente Raja was supported by a "Juan de la Cierva-Incorporación" Fellowship (Grant# IJC2020-044829-I) funded by MCIN/AEI /10.13039/501100011033 and by the European Union NextGenerationEU/PRTR, and by the grant PID2021-127294NA-I00 funded by MCIN/AEI/10.13039/501100011033 and by the European Union NextGenerationEU/PRTR.

Cambridge Elements ☰

Perception

James T. Enns
The University of British Columbia

Editor James T. Enns is Professor at the University of British Columbia, where he researches the interaction of perception, attention, emotion, and social factors. He has previously been editor of the *Journal of Experimental Psychology: Human Perception and Performance* and an associate editor at *Psychological Science, Consciousness and Cognition, Attention Perception & Psychophysics*, and *Visual Cognition*.

Advisory Board

Gregory Francis *Purdue University*

Kimberly Jameson *University of California, Irvine*

Tyler Lorig *Washington and Lee University*

Rob Gray *Arizona State University*

Salvador Soto-Faraco *Universitat Pompeu Fabra*

About the Series

The modern study of human perception includes event perception, bidirectional influences between perception and action, music, language, the integration of the senses, human action observation, and the important roles of emotion, motivation, and social factors. Each Element in the series combines authoritative literature reviews of foundational topics with forward-looking presentations of the recent developments on a given topic.

Cambridge Elements ≡

Perception

Elements in the Series

Printed in the United States
by Baker & Taylor Publisher Services